THE
ELVIS
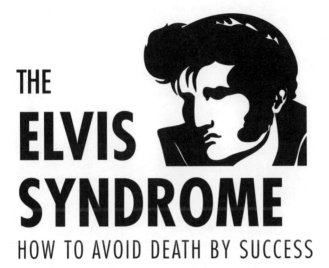
SYNDROME
HOW TO AVOID DEATH BY SUCCESS

JOHN Q. BAUCOM, Ph.D.

Fairview Press
Minneapolis

Published by Fairview Press, 2450 Riverside Ave. S., Minneapolis, MN 55454.

Library of Congress Cataloging-in-Publication Data

Baucom, John Q.
    The Elvis syndrome : how to avoid death by success / John Baucom.   p.   cm.
    Includes bibliographical references (p.   ) and index.
    ISBN 0-925190-38-1
    1. Self-destructive behavior. 2. Success--Psychological aspects. 3. Celebrities--Psychology. 4. Suicidal behavior.
I. Title.
RC569.5.S45B38   1995
158.7--dc20   95-19452
                                                                  CIP

First Printing: July 1995

Printed in the U.S.A.
99 98 97 96 95   7 6 5 4 3 2 1

Cover design: Circus Design

Publisher's note: Fairview Press publishes books and other materials related to the subjects of physical health, mental health, and chemical dependency. Its publications, including *The Elvis Syndrome*, do not necessarily reflect the philosophy of Fairview Hospital and Healthcare Services or their treatment programs.

To the life of Curtis and to the memory of Elvis Presley.

ACKNOWLEDGMENTS

There are various people that have contributed to this manuscript that I'd like to acknowledge. The first and foremost people are Bud and LA. It is not a cliché to say without them *The Elvis Syndrome* never would have been completed.

There are many others who have helped in various ways, including contributions of editing, quotations, and metaphors. My personal thanks go to Roy Glenn, Kathy Pascal, Floyd Celapino, Schaack Van Deusen, Bob Lanza, Barry Wagner, David Jarvis, Leah O'Neal, Lois Smith, John Thornton, Milton Vincent, Clairalyn, and Jeremy.

Contents

Chapter 1

ENDING UP ON LONELY STREET
AN INTRODUCTION TO
THE ELVIS SYNDROME

"You shall have joy, or you shall have power, said God:
you shall not have both."
—*Ralph Waldo Emerson, Journals 1842*

I can't take full credit for discovering the Elvis Syndrome. But neither can I share with you the name of a client in my private practice who first made me recognize its powerful existence. He's a country music performer, a star in his own right, who comes to see me for psychotherapy between the demands of road trips and recording sessions. This man, who I'll call "Curtis," idolizes Elvis Presley to the point of near-obsession. Despite that fascination, it took a long time for him to realize he was living a caricature of the King's life. But when he did, he also recognized that the insatiable hunger for success and the fear it wouldn't last had consumed him. He saw all too clearly that when the seductive whispers of fame begin their work on your psyche, you trip yourself up. You self-destruct without realizing what you're doing, or why. And in some cases, like Curtis, you're lucky to get out alive.

"I went through it all," Curtis told me one afternoon, leaning forward as if he were about to whisper a secret. "Booze, drugs, women, all sorts of craziness. The whole bit. In the beginning I had the best friends a man could want, a good family—everything. Then I just got too big for my britches and lost them all. After awhile I didn't have any real friends. Of course when I went on the road, everybody loved me. A year earlier, those same people wouldn't give me the time of day. So I figured now they liked me because I was a star. Hell, I ended up not trusting anyone. After awhile you get paranoid and just plum crazy. That's when you drink more. After awhile I nearly did myself in. I guess I'm really lucky to be alive."

Curtis's nearly fatal episode began with a bender one night on Nashville's Music Row. I sat in disbelief as he related the story. "I was using drugs. I was using people. I was using success. Man, I was a world-class user. I got so strung out on booze that I swear to God, I near about went crazy. I started drinking one night with some of my band members on Music Row. The next memory I have is four days later in a motel in Tucumcari, New Mexico. Can you believe that? Of all places in the country, I end up in Tucumcari! I have absolutely no memory of what happened during those four days. I was blacked out. I could have killed somebody for all I know. How the hell I got from Nashville, Tennessee, to Tucumcari, New Mexico, to this day I do not know. But it got my attention, I assure you of that."

At the very pinnacle of success, with all the money and fame he could want, Curtis was languishing in one of the last stages of advanced alcoholism. He managed to pull back from the brink with help from psychotherapy, his pastor, and his wife. But he wishes someone could have warned him early on about the perils of success. As is true in most cases, however, the very people who knew him best, didn't know how to help.

"See, my friends didn't know how to act around me. They figured I wouldn't want a thing to do with them, since I was famous. Me—I was honestly ashamed and embarrassed with all that money and attention. So we just drifted apart," Curtis explained. "I still hate all this, and I hate that people have to go through it. Somebody ought to get ahold of people before they get so big and let them know what they're getting into. I wish somebody could have done it with Elvis, for damn sure. He had all these people around him but I swear it's like he didn't need bodyguards, John, he needed life guards. He was destroyed. But then, maybe all of us are."

"You realize with finality that in some regard you would never be as good a man again."
—*F. Scott Fitzgerald*, The Crack-up Essays

In one of our early psychotherapy sessions, I pointed out the similarities between Curtis and Elvis. Flattered, Curtis brought some of his extensive Elvis memorabilia collection on his next visit. There was even a picture of Curtis and Elvis together, taken at one of "the King's" Las Vegas performances years earlier.

"Look here! You've gotta see this." Curtis offered me a copy of The New York Times dated Wednesday, August 17, 1977. "Elvis Presley Dies; Rock Singer Was Forty-Two," the headline glared. "Heart failure is cited by coroner—acclaim followed early scorn."

Curtis spoke up. "He didn't die by heart failure. And it wasn't accidental overdose either. I believe he OD'd on purpose. But who can figure? This guy really was the King. Even the Smithsonian Institution of all places, says Elvis was the most important influence in two hundred years of American music. He had it all—money, fame, success, talent—everything. Why would a man like that kill himself?" Curtis demanded. "Of course, I guess you could ask why I do some of the things I do as well."

I nodded silently, realizing I could ask myself the same question. Elvis Presley's death by success is shocking, yet he is not alone. Each of the following high-achieving people experienced death by success in some way. (A complete list is printed at the end of this book.)

Marilyn Monroe	Humphrey Bogart	James Dean
Richard Nixon	Janis Joplin	Howard Hughes
Rock Hudson	Jimi Hendrix	Hank Williams, Sr.
Ernest Hemingway	Vincent Van Gogh	Judy Garland
F. Scott Fitzgerald	W.C. Fields	Lenny Bruce
John Belushi	Andy Kaufman	Sam Kennison
Freddie Prinze	Lyle Alzedo	Kurt Cobain
Jim Henson	John Candy	River Phoenix
Pee-Wee Herman*	Jim Morrison	Len Bias
Jim Fixx	Jim Jones	David Koresh
Cheyene Brando		

(*Paul Reubens is still alive. The death of Pee-Wee Herman is discussed in chapter nine.)

And think about how these people "Elvised out" (As the manuscript for *The Elvis Syndrome* progressed, it became natural for us to refer to individuals who were sabotaging themselves as "Elvising out.")

Gary Hart	Jimmy Swaggart	Jim Bakker
Pete Rose	Wilbur Mills	Rob Lowe
Mickey Monus	Ted Kennedy	James Watt
Hank Williams Jr.	Derrick Sanderson	Willie Nelson
Martin Siegel	Ivan Boesky	Steve Howe
Dennis Levine	Leona Helmsley	Chuck Berry
Michael Milken	Jerry Lee Lewis	Brian Wilson
Sam Pierce	Marion Barry	Paul Reubens
George Jones	Greta Garbo	David Crosby
Darryl Strawberry	Mike Tyson	O.J. Simpson

As you look at these two lists, you can probably think of others. Now think of your own personal acquaintances. Friends who have succeeded, then failed miserably. The police officer who lost his job for drunken driving. The teacher who was fired for having a sexual relationship with a student. The bartender who struggled, scrimped and saved to buy his own business, then drank away the profits. You may even see a time when you have sabotaged your own success. It's startling that people from such varied backgrounds as hockey player Derrick Sanderson, Phar-Mor founder Mickey Monus and former secretary of Housing and Urban Development Sam Pierce could all end up "down at the end of Lonely Street." But it's downright frightening to realize you could end up joining them.

"The moral flabbiness of the bitch goddess success. That — with the squalid cash interpretation put on the word success — is our national disgrace."
— William James, letter to H.G. Wells, September 11, 1906

Before you rule out that possibility, consider how the gospel-singing Elvis viewed success early in his career. After his first national appearances with Ed Sullivan and Steve Allen, Elvis reportedly told his friends, "Y'all don't worry none. The people in New York and Hollywood, they ain't gonna change me a bit."

Contrast that Elvis with the picture Curtis paints of the singer's final days:

"On the night of his death, poor old Elvis had been reduced to this. Now listen. This is really sick. When he got ready to go to bed he would get this envelope marked with the words— 'First Attack.' Inside was about a dozen pills and three syringes. The pills were mostly downers. And the syringes had Demerol, Valium, and God-knows-what in them. Well anyway, he would down these pills, and then get all three shots in the back of his shoulder blades. Then, he'd race to see if he could get three cheeseburgers and six milk shakes—literally six milk shakes— down before he passed out." Curtis shook his head back and forth and smiled weakly.

"Sometimes they'd have to reach down his throat and rake out what was left of the cheeseburger so he wouldn't choke to death. Four hours later he'd get his second envelope and two or three hours after that, his third. When it came time to get up, he'd take speed, uppers, and whatever else. Now this is how this man lived—if you call that living—his last days. And there were people all around him. But they couldn't stop it."

This is a phenomenon we see all too frequently in families. A teenager tries to commit suicide, is heavily involved with drugs or alcohol abuse, or is in the advanced stages of bulimia or anorexia. And the parents say, "We didn't know." Like Elvis, the teenager's behavior is a silent cry for help. But we tend to overlook things in those we love. We ignore that bottle of scotch hidden in the closet, the food binges, the withdrawal. Changes in behavior don't have to be dramatic to be important. The most dangerous occur slowly, almost insidiously. And the more successful we become, the more leeway other people appear willing to give. It's as if they assume mastery of a job is the same as mastery of life.

The history of humankind is filled with deadly accounts of highly gifted people who have thought they had established mastery. Self-destructiveness is not only a possibility, but some suggest, your birthright. By biblical accounts the first people on earth, Adam and Eve, were given everything they possibly needed for happiness. Yet they chose the one option that destroyed everything they had. Similarly, the story of Moses leading the Jews from bondage is filled with accounts of self-sabotage and self-defeating behavior. King David continually ran into trouble because of his own self-destructive drives.

One of the most curious accounts of this phenomenon comes from the ancient Roman empire. The custom was attributed to "appeasing the gods." But the series of customs actually helped high achievers of the period avoid self-sabotage. Roman conquering generals were granted incredible status by both leaders and citizens. Elaborate and expensive parades were conducted to celebrate the conquering hero. However, as he rode on his chariot, and enjoyed the adulation of his followers, the general was accompanied by a slave standing alongside him holding a golden crown. The slave's job was to repeat over and over, "Look behind you and remember you're a man." At other times the slave would whisper, "Fame is fleeting, fame is fleeting." Apparently, the custom was practiced throughout the Roman empire. It helped the hero keep his perspective.

Julius Caesar, the most renowned Roman of all, was rewarded for conquering Gaul with the most elaborate parade in Roman history. But even Caesar was expected to take his success with a few grains of salt. As his chariot proceeded down the street, a group of unimpressed soldiers chanted, "Urbani, servate axores; moechum calvum adducimus." Roughly translated, this was the equivalent of: "Romans, lock up your wives, we are bringing back the bald adulterer." His head may have been bald, but it wasn't likely to swell. As bizarre as the custom sounds, it probably helped some Roman heroes expand not only their life expectancy, but their success as well.

"There's always something about your success that displeases even your best friends."
— Oscar Wilde, Irish poet and playwright

Though Julius Caesar may not have self-destructed from a swelled head, many others have struggled with this problem. One of my first professional experiences with this occurred with a woman I still call "MDWIFE," although I've known her over a dozen years. MDWIFE was the moniker on her vanity license plate when we first met. The license plate was symbolically part of her problem—the same problem that contributes to the Elvis Syndrome. It's a story you've probably heard before, about someone else.

MDWIFE had worked and financially supported her husband through college and medical school. Her husband, whose first two initials are poetically M.D., was a tremendous student and excelled in school. But he didn't have much time for her or their marriage. Unfortunately, this is quite common for medical students. She seldom complained and they both pitched in. It was a sacrifice, they figured, but the payoff would come. Finally he finished the laborious requirements of school, internship, and residency. He was exhausted by it, but immediately entered a surgical group practice and soon was earning substantial money.

These two had grown up together. They became friends in junior high school, started dating in the tenth grade and were engaged by their senior year. They got married while in college. She had seen M.D. through a lot of tough times. To her he was a normal guy. He lost his temper, used the toilet, and had some poor personal hygiene habits, just like the rest of us. Most of their lives, she treated him as a normal guy, and that was fine. But then he became a surgeon. She describes it as if someone had waved a magic wand, and suddenly everything changed. He wasn't any longer just a husband. Now he was—*a doctor*!

Nurses catered to him. Patients worshiped him. Children adored him. Hospital administrators kissed up to him. Pharmaceutical sales representatives wined and dined him. People lived and died at the end of his magic wand—his scalpel. But when he returned home, he was just plain old "Matt." Not a god. Not a doctor. Not a miracle-worker. But simply Matt, a husband. And unfortunately, he couldn't handle it.

To give him credit, he persisted. He didn't *try* to be a husband. He simply persisted at being married. In response, she became involved in medical auxiliary and played the doctor's wife role. They remained married by his account, five years and two children longer than they should have. He was generous with his money, which became a problem later. He bought her new furs, a new Mercedes, and the new vanity license plate. But he gave up on the relationship. "She just doesn't treat me right, " he complained. "And besides, her weight problem bothers me."

His scrub nurse, however, did treat him right. She treated him like a doctor—almost *like a god*. MDWIFE treated him like a husband. There is a big difference. MD didn't have a Roman slave following him around to humble him and pretty soon his swelled head got him in a great deal of trouble. He became deified and began to believe he was above the rules. People treated him like a god and MD decided he was one. He got his scrub nurse pregnant, decided to divorce MDWIFE, and attempted to deify himself in the wrong courtroom. A circuit court judge taught him differently. MD got his scrub nurse, who of course treats him like a husband now. She also has her own weight problem. MDWIFE got everything else. She also got a new vanity license plate: "XMDWFE."

In some cases deification can have a humorous twist. In others the result is deadly, not only to the one being deified but to others as well. It can begin innocently or even benignly. Both Jim Jones and David Koresh were clergy. They were elevated by themselves and their followers mutually. Over time each man was responsible not only for his own death, but literally dozens of others. It's a dangerous process. Deification is one of the prime elements in the Elvis Syndrome. Anytime you begin to believe you're a deity or that normal rules no longer apply, you're headed rapidly toward the Elvis Syndrome. This is of such importance it's discussed in detail in a later chapter.

MDWIFE also brought up another element I find in mammoth proportions among those headed toward the Elvis Syndrome—depression. When she first came for psychotherapy she was about two weeks postpartum. Ten days earlier she had given birth to their second child. She described herself as experiencing severe depression literally hours after delivery. This had also occurred, she claimed, after the birth of her first child and lasted for several weeks. Many women experience postpartum depression. Some experts say it's biological, others say it's psychological and even others say it's a combination. Regardless, it's a common occurrence.

There are other kinds of blues people often experience. Anyone who has been in a school play can describe a similar emotional slump after it's over. Athletes have described to me an equally intense downswing after the season or after important competitions regardless of the outcome. Accountants have reported it at the end of tax season. There is a post-Christmas slump, the post-political campaign blues, the post-project let-down, the post-concert blahs. I've heard this called everything from the "done-did-it" blues, to post-performance malaise, and post-event melancholia. It is actually a form of the Elvis Syndrome.

Regardless of what you call it, the phenomenon is quite common. It occurs upon completion of something perceived as vastly important. Energy, attention and intensity are focused on the event. The nature of the event is irrelevant. It's the *attention* that's important. It's the *intensity*, the *energy*, the *focus*. And when all of that is taken away . . . there's an emptiness. The blues. Depression. A void. It's pure emptiness. Multiply this experience several hundred times in frequency and intensity and you begin to approximate the Elvis Syndrome. Over the course of a career, a roller coaster impact occurs. A roller coaster is fun occasionally, but nobody wants to live on one. Eventually, some people are willing to jump off the roller coaster just to avoid the ride. Others engage in other self-destructing activities to end the madness. One of the reasons there are so many suicides among entertainers, athletes, and comedians is because it is an expedient way to get off the roller coaster. The natural question in response to this statement is: Why doesn't it happen more frequently?

> *"Success has ruined many a man."*
> —*Benjamin Franklin,* Poor Richard's Almanac

Over time I learned there are many important components of the Elvis Syndrome. One of the most common is the absolute obsession to achieve. This may sound like a positive trait, and in some cases it can be, initially. High performers give one hundred percent. Whatever they do, they give it their all. The greater their ego and need for recognition, the more dangerous their compulsion. If they succeed, it will be grand. But if they fail, it will be grand as well. Their compulsion to do well is an addiction as real and potentially harmful as drugs.

Like any structure, success must be built on a foundation. Curtis originally built his success on the foundation of his family and close friends, his strong social network. Eventually, his focus narrowed, and he became obsessed with success. He ignored and ultimately forgot about his social network—the very basis of his success. Like a drug addict searching for the ultimate high, he continued to obsess about success. Striving, achieving, and succeeding became a fixation. Meanwhile the foundation crumbled. And when it did, the entire family expended a tremendous amount of energy to rebuild the foundation, yet they still had tremendous difficulty. This can happen to anyone, not just the famous.

Consider the bus driver who is arrested for drunken driving. His drinking may have had nothing to do with his responsibilities as a bus driver. But if he loses his license, he's lost the one thing needed to continue his career. One of my clients, a brilliant young woman on a full academic scholarship, got caught shoplifting a ten-dollar wallet. Her crime was not one of need. She had several hundred dollars on her when she was apprehended. The Elvis Syndrome also afflicts young women who struggle with obesity. They work hard, starve themselves to death, and almost go crazy trying to lose weight, so they can feel attractive. But the minute they begin getting close to a man, they get scared and gain all the weight back. All of these people ignored the foundation on which their achievement was based. When one is fixated obsessively on success, it's far too easy to lose perspective.

Curtis helped explain this. He became so intoxicated by fame that it blinded him to everything but the next concert. Like a drug addict, he became obsessed by his next fix. As he described the sensation, he leaned toward me and in almost a whisper said,

"Let me tell you something, John. I do this now because it's enjoyable. Singing, writing, entertaining. But it wasn't always like that. There was a time when I was a concert junkie. I could not live without the fix of going on tour. When I was off the road I was like a heroin addict in withdrawal. I did it because I had to have the rush of stepping out on stage. Hundreds, sometimes thousands, of people applauding. Making them laugh, cry, dance, move. I swear to God it was the greatest sex I ever had! I was definitely addicted. Back then I didn't do it because I wanted to. I did it because it was the only time I felt good about myself. It wasn't the money, though there was lots of it. I did it because I had to. It got me high, man. It was definitely my drug, and I'm here to tell you there are lots of addicts. In entertainment. In sports. In business. It's everywhere, don't kid yourself."

> *"Fame always brings loneliness.*
> *Success is as ice cold and lonely as the North Pole."*
> *— Vicky Baum,* Grand Hotel

The more you understand the Elvis Syndrome, the more you may recognize a personal tendency toward self-destruction. You may be your own biggest obstacle to success. Because you don't take drugs or get drunk, you may believe you're fine. But success may seduce you into other behaviors equally dangerous. For instance, you may wolf down a quick greasy burger at your desk rather than go out for a healthy lunch. The rationale: You don't have the time to take a real lunch break. You may work long hours consistently, despite the strain it's putting on your marriage or children. Perhaps you find busy work to fill your time instead of important projects. You figure you'll wait until the time is right to complete the important ones. If so, you're already creating stumbling blocks. You may shake your head and wonder at the likes of John Belushi, Jim Morrison or Marilyn Monroe. But realize there are millions of others who suffer the same affliction and fate and get no attention at all. One of them could be you.

Virtually everyone faces the Elvis Syndrome at some point. When it's your turn, will you be destroyed, or overcome it? The answer lies in the intensity of the "addiction." And there are a variety of factors that determine its intensity. Though a more comprehensive picture is presented later in this book, a summary of some of the significant factors is presented here to give you a beginning level of understanding. Though they're difficult to quantify, the factors include: talent, ambition, narcissism, emotional equipment and social network.

The first three factors are risk-oriented. Talent is vital to success, but people with little talent who rate high in narcissism and ambition may still suffer from the Elvis Syndrome. Narcissism is extremely important. For these purposes it is defined as the need for attention and a desire to be the center of focus. Ambition combines the desire to succeed with the self-discipline and the work ethic needed to achieve success.

The other factors contribute to stability. Emotional equipment is an assessment of how well-equipped psychologically one is to handle the challenges of success. Some danger signs include: success guilt, a suspicion of others, and isolation. More obvious signs include drug abuse, alcohol abuse, and an increased separation from family and friends.

The final factor, the strength of your social network, may determine whether you survive or succumb to the Elvis Syndrome. The social network of a successful person may be made up of a few honest friends, but usually he or she is surrounded by "groupies." The downfall of boxer Mike Tyson is a good example of the function of a strong social network. When Mike's adopted father and manager, Cus D'Amato, was alive and had the original management team supporting the champ, Tyson was not only successful but also disciplined enough to stay out of trouble. He was agreeable, respectful, and conducted himself maturely in interviews. After D'Amato's death, the carefully chosen network built around Tyson crumbled and his deterioration began. Under new management, and with a new entourage, Tyson stepped over the line. He was imprisoned for rape and his career was over for awhile.

A healthy network is one in which friends are honest with a potentially self-destructive individual. They are willing to intervene, even dramatically, if necessary. Though such networks are difficult to find, they do exist. Emotional equipment and social networks act as "parachutes." They reduce the risk of self-destructiveness. The good news is that emotional equipment and social networks (addressed later in this book) can be built.

> *"Fame is like a river that beareth up things light and swollen and drowns things weighty and solid."*
> —*Francis Bacon*, Of Ceremonies and Respects

A strong social network could have helped Michael Jackson avoid his problems. During the time Curtis was in psychotherapy with me, Jackson had denied charges of child molestation and negotiated a financial settlement out of court. Whether guilty or not, Jackson apparently had engaged in some behavior that, at a minimum, questioned his good judgment. Curtis brought up the case during a session, suggesting Jackson suffered from the same need for lifeguards Elvis did.

"Of course," Curtis continued. "What Michael really needs is some serious help growing up. I mean this is a classic case of somebody who never got to be a kid. I think what Michael really wanted was simply to be a little boy. He never got to have a childhood. When he was five years old he was out making a living, for God's sake. Now he wants to go back and be a kid. He wanted to have a slumber party. He just wanted some kids to sleep over. I doubt he did anything different than my own kids have done. I definitely don't think he had sex with those boys. The trouble is, though, what he's done is out of line. He ought to have somebody there—one of those lifeguards we talked about earlier—who'd pick him up and shake him and say, 'Michael don't you see what you're doing? Man, this is gonna look bad. I'm not going to let this destroy you. I'm going to take you to someone who can help. I'm gonna help you save your life.' This is just another case of somebody's fame wearing them out. I really believe it's Elvis all over again, and it scares me to death.

"They said Michael's addicted to pain killers. So was Elvis. Michael's isolated. So was Elvis. Michael's surrounded by people who want to please him. So was Elvis. Man! There are so many similarities. And now he's married Elvis' daughter. Honest to God, this is just too strange for me.

"But it happens to just about everybody in this business. I know of dozens or even hundreds of people in the music business this has happened to. And politics and industry. Actors and actresses and sports stars. Man, it's everywhere! And the folks around them, and the managers and agents, and all these people—they do just every single thing they can to save the person's career but not a damn thing to save their life. And then when somebody does try to help, the star or athlete or singer, or whoever it is, he fires them. I mean, the whole thing is just sick. It's a brave new world, huh?"

During this time in his therapy Curtis began to wonder whether the streak of self-destructiveness was a natural part of each person. I looked in my old textbooks to see whether I could find a name for this particular kind of behavior. Though there was nothing directly related, I found one humorous term, *nike-phobia*. Much to the chagrin of the people who market sneakers from Oregon, it was described as "fear of victory."

This is the truth about death by success: Deep within the recesses of your unconscious mind there's a mechanism that somehow prevents you from doing your best. For some, it's like a thermostat, adjusted to a success comfort zone. If achievement occurs outside its limit, positively or negatively, a mechanism kicks in and brings you back within comfortable boundaries.

Drugs and alcohol contribute to the Elvis Syndrome. So can publicity, the press and praise. Success itself may affect you adversely. Why? Because virtually all of us have difficulty dealing with success. Experts speculate that seventy percent of all people doubt success will last. Most feel guilt or embarrassment when they succeed to a high level. Others simply have no role model on how to handle success.

After listening to Curtis, I began to do some investigating of my own into Elvis Presley's background. I discovered he was very close to his mother, and those who knew him say he never got over her death. Elvis seemed to carry guilt about his success, along with overwhelming sadness about his mother's death. He ultimately died at approximately the same age as his mother, on approximately the same date, and of the same cause. It is almost as if he wouldn't give himself permission to outlive her.

I shared this insight with Curtis, who teased me about being a closet Elvis freak. He wondered whether I'd been to Graceland to burn candles. While I didn't share Curtis's fascination for Elvis, I did begin to see a strong correlation between Elvis' death by success and the way millions of others destroy their lives. The Elvis Syndrome is rooted in the unconscious mind, begins in childhood, and is influenced by family. One rarely notes the danger signs until adolescence. If not treated, it can be fatal.

Curtis had only one question about my developing theory: "Is there a cure? Is there some way to get off Lonely Street?" The answer is yes. There is a cure. It can work for millionaires on Wall Street, for average Joes trying to make top salesmen, and it can work for you. But it requires facing up to some difficult facts. The first step is to use the following pages to see just how much the Elvis Syndrome affects your life. The second step is to begin a journal to chart your own progress.

JOURNAL SESSION

Directions: You will benefit more while reading this book if you take notes or discuss your responses to the material in writing. After each chapter, you'll be asked to think about episodes in your own life and write your responses. If you complete these assignments in detail, you may see recurring self-destructive patterns in your life that have been unrecognized. This information will help you gain insight and avoid self-sabotage.

1. Make a list of the occasions when you have "self-destructed, " or been responsible for sabotaging your own success. Consider beginning with high school, choosing at least one example from each four- or five-year period of your adult life from adolescence until today. For example, choose one experience from your high school years; one from college years or early twenties; one from early years of marriage, etc. Expand on each example. Try to isolate patterns you encounter.

2. Generally speaking, do you consider yourself a candidate for the Elvis Syndrome? Why or why not? Discuss this with

someone who knows you well. What is his or her feedback? In that person's opinion, are you a candidate for the Elvis Syndrome?

3. What is the greatest loss you have suffered or the greatest price you have paid when it comes to sabotaging your own success? Choose the most dramatic example or the greatest loss you have experienced by self-sabotage. Explain it in detail and define what aspects were caused by your own behavior. Note those aspects for which you were directly responsible.

4. List any miniature Elvis Syndrome experiences you may have experienced. Your list might include post-partum depression, "after-the-play blahs," etc. Discuss in writing your feelings during one of those experiences. Discuss how the increased intensity and frequency of those experiences might affect your ability to cope with everyday problems.

CHECKLIST

Directions: Rate each trait on a scale from zero (it does not apply to me at all) to four (it applies a great deal of the time.)

____1. I have been told by others or believe myself that "I am my own worst enemy" or that "I am self-destructive."

____2. I measure my success by earnings, promotions, or by the approval of someone above me.

____3 What others think is extremely important to me.

____4. I feel driven to achieve. It's almost as if there's a force outside of me that drives me to achieve.

____5. On many occasions I have sped in my car, far too fast for road conditions.

____6. I have few or no friends who are close to me other than business associates.

____7. I experience angry outbursts that seem to surface for no reason.

____8. People describe me as being "on the way up" the ladder.

____9. Alcohol or other drugs have created problems for me.

___10. Others have suggested that I drink too much.

___11. People have accused me of being self-centered, selfish, narcissistic.

___12. I have trouble keeping emotional commitments to others.

___13. I have experienced marital problems or problems with intimate relationships.

___14. Few people know the "real" me.

___15. It is very important to me that I be "right."

___16. There are a limited number of things that interest me.

___17. My parents have or had problems with alcohol or other drugs.

___18. I could be described as having a great deal of talent.

___19. I've been told by more than one person that I have a big ego.

___20. I'm seldom if ever satisfied with my achievements.

___21. People could describe me as an adventure-seeker.

___22. I have difficulty trusting other people, even on the job.

___23. I have experimented sexually on more than one occasion.

___24. Other people could describe me as ruthless.

___25. I have been divorced (or its equivalent) at least once.

___TOTAL

How to Score Yourself: Add your score together. The closer you get to one hundred, the higher your risk for the Elvis Syndrome.

Below 49: Don't quit your day job, if you have one!

50-59: You probably will be successful and avoid the Elvis Syndrome.

60-69: Re-examine your life. It's not too late to avoid trouble.

70-79: Be cautious. You're headed for trouble.

80-89: See a professional. You're in trouble.

90-100: Call me, or fly to Chattanooga. You're in serious or imminent danger.

Chapter 2

<u>CHECKING INTO HEARTBREAK HOTEL</u>
BEGINNING TO EXPERIENCE
THE ELVIS SYNDROME

"Whom the gods wish to destroy they first call promising."
— Cyril Connelly

It had been several weeks since I had spoken to Curtis. LA gave me a message to return his call between appointments. I was curious to find out what was going on. After several rings, Curtis answered.

"Hey, man! How's it going?" I asked. "It's been awhile. I got your message a moment ago."

"Dr. John," he responded. "Listen, man. It's good to hear from you. I've only got a minute right now, but I've got to tell you something. Does the name Michael English mean anything to you?"

"No," I answered. "It sounds familiar. But I don't recognize it. Why? Should I?"

"Well, not necessarily," Curtis hedged. "But you'll recognize it tomorrow. He's taking the exit to Heartbreak Hotel. Michael won the GMA [Gospel Music Awards] Singer-of-the-Year Award a week or so ago. Tomorrow he's going to resign and give up his award due to—let's say—sexual impropriety. I think it'll be in the announcement. Can you believe it? Man, how much more of this can the world tolerate?"

I was stunned. "I don't know what to say. Is this all going to come out tomorrow?"

"Yeah. I think there'll be a press conference." Curtis cleared his throat. "The print media probably won't have anything out 'til the day after tomorrow. It'll get front-page coverage in most of the country. He's pretty big, John. TV will be covering it for sure."

"And this guy just got Gospel Singer of the Year?" I asked.

"Yeah," Curtis coughed. "Let's put it this way. He is to gospel what Garth Brooks is to country. He's big. But now he's history. Can you believe this?"

"Yeah." I nodded silently. "I can believe it. Another one Elvised out, huh?"

"Well," Curtis drawled. "Like Tennessee Ernie Ford used to say, 'If the left one don't get you, the right one will.' Something always gets them, John. I think maybe there needs to be a new kind of psychology—the study of people who self-destruct or something like that. Maybe even better would be the psychology of stars, the psychology of success. We're definitely a screwed-up bunch."

> *"Success is the one unpardonable sin against one's fellows."*
> *—Ambrose Bierce*

High-achieving people (HAPs) present society with unique problems. Psychology, psychiatry, and sociology were based on studies of "average" people with average aspirations. Therefore woefully little is actually known about high achievers. Their problems are magnified and exploited by media but not investigated or understood by the behavioral sciences. In fact, one of the great failures of the behavioral sciences has been to provide an understanding of what mental health is at all. The tomes of research available focus on sickness. The absence of sickness is then considered normal. The assumption that normal is healthy is one of the fundamental errors mental-health professionals have made. It is a central flaw in psychotherapy. To further assume that normal principles apply to those who achieve at higher-than-normal levels is an equally disastrous mistake. Perhaps Curtis is correct in suggesting a new science. Certainly what we currently have is inadequate.

A HAP's journey can be understood by looking at a typical evolution. Whether entertainer, athlete, or executive, the steps are fairly similar. *Stage one* is education and preparation. Education does not necessarily imply schooling. It can be education of other types. *Stage two* is early skill refinement. For athletes, this may begin by playing Little League or high school sports. *Stage three* is intense training or skill refinement (college sports, for example; or with a musician it might be an intense period playing with relatively unknown groups). *Stage four* is initial success. At this point a HAP would (a) level out and grow comfortable with the achievement level; (b) begin self sabotaging or diversify into other areas; or (c) enter *stage five*, called exponential success. Afterwards, the HAP can develop into *stage six*, where the inevitable death by success occurs.

The journey of a HAP may be measured in decades spent at one of various stages. The instant success we imagine is actually a phenomenon of instant media exposure, not instant talent. The instant exposure usually brings immediate fame and often financial rewards. However, it also brings equally intense risk. Instant exposure does not bring with it a set of instant directions on how to handle it. Some HAPs, but only a few, are able to face it in a healthy way. Most check into Heartbreak Hotel. What makes the difference?

> *"I can't give you a surefire formula for success, but I can give you a formula for failure: Try to please everybody all the time."*
> —Herbert Bayard Swope

The *American Heritage Dictionary* defines success as "the achievement of something desired, planned or attempted . . . the gaining of fame or prosperity." Webster's New World Dictionary defines it as "result; outcome; a favorable or satisfactory outcome or result." Dictionaries don't agree on how success is defined and, unfortunately, neither does society. The definitions most widely accepted are focused primarily on the accumulation of status and things.

Lewis Richmond's article in the May 16, 1994, issue of *Fortune* magazine defines success as achieving "the three R's—respect, recognition, and remuneration." Respect from peers and colleagues was considered important. Recognition, primarily for achievement, also was highly rated. But remuneration—money and possessions was most important of all. The October 1993 issue of *Esquire* was devoted entirely to famous people's thoughts on success. Most of the comments were similar to *Fortune* magazine's article. Success was primarily defined as "possessing . . . house, car, boat, jewelry, and other creature comforts." *Esquire* described Americans as being obsessed with proving their success to others with possessions. The Lou Harris polling organization did an exhaustive study on how Americans define success. Their results agreed with the descriptions above.

Society is fascinated with success. *Lifestyles of the Rich and Famous* has become an institution. But at the same time society has a love-hate relationship with those who succeed. Great Britain's obsession with the royal family is a classic example. The world's focus on Michael Jackson and O. J. Simpson are other illustrations. Somehow, as a society we are attracted and repulsed simultaneously by high-achieving people. The superstar level of success is apparently too much for most people to accept. It's as if by achieving this status, the HAPs have violated the status quo of mediocrity in the most vile of ways. Misery doesn't love company. It loves miserable company. Society needs heroes and elevates people to that status. And then that same society glories in the hero's fall as if it makes the masses feel better. From the crucifixion of Jesus Christ to the pathetic forty-three-mile caravan down the freeways of Los Angeles in June, 1994, society has had tremendous difficulty tolerating success. And apparently we have even more difficulty understanding and accepting those who succeed.

To understand the evolution of the Elvis Syndrome, look first at the dominant attitudes and avenues leading there. Different people take different paths to the Elvis Syndrome and some take more than one. Tragically, Elvis himself took them all.

> *"Some people would like him (Albert Schweitzer) a lot better now,*
> *if only he had suffered more."*
> *— Kurt Vonnegut, Jr.*

"I don't know. Hell, John, you tell me. You're supposed to be the expert." Topanga Jack leaned forward, his eyes focusing intensely. He looked beyond me and spoke slowly, meticulously choosing each word. "I can buy anything I want. I never have to work another day in my life. I've got cars, houses, planes, women. You name it. This is supposed to be success, by anybody's standards. *But if I'm so damned successful, why am I miserable?* Now, explain that to me if you can."

I listened silently and nodded as Topanga Jack spoke. He was a true self-made multimillionaire and had acquired it all the old-fashioned way. During the time he was building his business he slept very little, destroyed two marriages, and became a workaholic. He set his goals and did it on his own. Topanga Jack had accepted society's definition of success, followed all the rules, and achieved. But like most other HAPs, he ended up unhappy. While the rules had led to the external trappings of success, the internal equivalent had been ignored.

"Is it true?" Topanga Jack spoke again after a brief silence. "Is it true that Ernest Hemingway said, *'A man is not a man until he commits suicide'*? Did he really say that? Because if he did, I understand what he meant!"

Topanga Jack described the most common attitude of the Elvis Syndrome. He had set aside his definition of success and played by society's rules. He had concentrated on success but not on contentment or happiness. Then when faced with the dilemma of having all the things, he looked inside himself and still found misery. Topanga Jack could find no logical explanation to what he was experiencing, and like other HAPs he assumed something must be wrong with him. He had everything, he reasoned, but still was unhappy. He had it all. Therefore he assumed happiness was unachievable and consequently became hopeless. But Topanga Jack had never focused on happiness. He focused on success constantly and assumed that's where happiness would be. Because of similar logic, many HAPs end up attempting suicide, or struggling with alcoholism and depression. They feel hopeless and echo Topanga Jack: *"If I'm so successful, why am I so miserable?"*

Like most other HAPs, Topanga Jack believed success lies "out there"—that it's something you can achieve and actually possess. Once obtained, then you own it. You can own many of the external possessions. Yet they don't result in internal happiness. Most HAPs feel they have followed all the rules, yet when the internal emotions don't change they begin to think of themselves as failures. "If I can't be happy when I've got all this, then something's hellaciously wrong with me," Topanga Jack later continued. Something was wrong. He'd focused on the wrong goal. He thought he could own contentment just as he owned cars and homes.

There are two other problems with this attitude. If you consider success to be only external, you automatically set yourself up for failure. If you take this approach, you can only be as happy as your last performance. This is true regardless of whether your performance is a song, touchdown, or sale. Allowing your feelings to be defined by the performance is to die when the performance sags. Additionally, you can fall into the trap of "more." You must be better than last time. More is expected. The old standards no longer work. So you strive and achieve the impossible standards, or eventually give up and try medicating yourself with drugs. Because in reality you can't always do more. Finally, if you follow this path, you become subject to the approval of others. Society, at best, is fickle. At the worst, society wants you to fail. Applause eventually stops. You have to live with yourself beyond the applause. The ways to do this are discussed later in this book.

"A tendency to self destruction seems to be inherent in the overdeveloped human brain."
—A. T. W. Simeons

As I was leaving the locker room after working out, I overheard a conversation that embarrassed me, even within the context of a male locker room. Two grown men—both in their fifties—were arguing over whose was biggest.

"Mine is," one explained, "It's quite obvious. Somebody get me a ruler." I couldn't see them and was glad at the moment. It was humiliating enough as it was. Even though the language gets rough in locker rooms, I really didn't expect this sort of behavior.

"Actually," the other voice began, "you may be right. Yours may be longer. But mine's bigger around. The actual mass of mine is greater by far."

"Bull," the other voice answered. "Where's Baucom? We'll ask him who's biggest."

I slammed my locker and began to hasten down the aisle. They headed me off at the pass and asked me to decide whose was bigger. Those two guys competed at everything, but this contest was crazy even by my standards. The question, incidentally, was who had the biggest scar from bypass surgery!

The most frequently socially-defined role of men has been to master the environment. In the early stages of society's development that meant using the environment to provide for your family. Today it means a bit more than having the biggest bypass scar, but to most men it does mean being the best. Determining "whose is biggest" involves comparison and competition. The locker-room discussion actually did occur as portrayed. It also demonstrates that the male role really hasn't changed much over the years. It still revolves around competing to determine who will win.

The sad reality is that the conversation above actually portrays the insanity of the adult male. This is one reason death by success occurs more often among males. The fact that two well-educated and highly successful men would compete over an operation that could have cost their lives demonstrates how insane it really is. Since I know both of these men, I can say it was the Elvis Syndrome that caused their surgery anyway. The fact they turn their scars into contests illustrates they haven't learned to avoid the Elvis Syndrome in the future. I did speak with each of them and their wives separately much later to express my concern with the attitude they demonstrated. The role these two men played, and the male role in general, is a problem.

Nevertheless Elvis Syndrome is not determined by gender. It's determined by the role the person plays and the way he or she handles such things. Traditionally more men have had leadership roles, so they've had more opportunity for success—and resultantly more opportunity to experience death by success. Women, much to their credit, have had more nurturing personality characteristics throughout time. Their roles in society have shifted dramatically over the past fifty years. Still, it remains a more nurturing responsibility, especially regarding child rearing. As women adapt to more traditionally defined workplace responsibilities, the incidence of the Elvis Syndrome among them will increase. Coronary problems, suicide, and alcoholism already have been increasing among women.

You only have to scan recent headlines of Tonya Harding, Lorena Bobbitt, and others to realize women already suffer from the Elvis Syndrome. And as women continue to achieve more, their risk of succumbing to the Elvis Syndrome increases simultaneously. Marilyn Monroe, Janis Joplin, and Leona Helmsly are all examples of this phenomenon. The fact is, the moment men or women take on any high-performance role, they immediately become candidates for the Elvis Syndrome. The importance is not gender, but performance.

"Success and failure are both difficult to endure. Along with success comes drugs, divorce, fornication, bullying, travel, meditation, medication, depression, neurosis, and suicide. With failure comes failure."
—Joseph Heller

Regardless of societal factors, the journey to Heartbreak Hotel is ultimately an internal one. The HAP, above all people, internalizes societal expectations. He or she then chooses the path, often semiconsciously. The question ultimately focuses on how death by success can happen with such frequency. Though there are many contributing factors discussed throughout this book, there are seven theoretical avenues that result in the Elvis Syndrome. Some are unmarked cow-paths. Others are speedways. But they all lead to the same destination. Reaching this undesirable destination may depend on your comfort zone. Comfort-zone problems, and your success thermostat, are the most frequent avenues leading to the Elvis Syndrome.

Bob, an All-American field-goal kicker his senior year in college, had tremendous comfort-zone problems. Though he looked more like a nose tackle, short and square-bodied, he actually was a tremendous kicker. In fact, his senior year he was one of the top-rated kickers in the country. Somehow *he* ended up checking into Heartbreak Hotel.

"I guess, if the truth were known, I blew it." Bob was explaining what had become of his career. "College was one thing. Really it was a breeze. I expected to excel there. But somehow, in my mind, the pros were way up here." He drew an imaginary line above his head. "And I was still a country boy somewhere down here." He gestured at waist level.

A reality many people can't understand is that success actually is far more stressful than failure. Holmes and Rhae did initial research and writing on stress. They pointed out that positive changes such as job promotion and salary increase are quite stressful. Most people mistakenly assume it will be easy to cope with success. In fact, the mere possibility of facing success is so aversive to some people they prevent it all together. Somehow, success on a large scale is outside their comfort zone.

Major success was certainly outside Bob's comfort zone. Everyone has a comfort zone of achievement and a success thermostat. At some point in your life you set this thermostat. It probably occurs quite early. Unless you adjust the thermostat, it will dictate your achievement level regardless of talent. It functions identically to the thermostat in your home. If the temperature reaches outside a designated range, your furnace or air conditioner will automatically come on. The temperature is then adjusted back within the comfort zone. Similarly, you have a success comfort zone. If your achievement falls below it, a mechanism kicks on and you adjust. At the same time, if you succeed beyond the thermostat setting, it kicks on again and cools your performance down to a comfortable level.

In Bob's case, the thermostat was set too low and he sabotaged an opportunity to play professional football. One factor in lowering his setting had to do with belief . Bob perceived the pros as "way up there" and himself as far below that level. The other factors were social. Bob had grown up in the rural south and never lived more than a few miles from where he was born. During our sessions he finally realized and admitted that moving away from home, especially to a large city, was more than he could handle. The possibility of spending winters in Green Bay, Chicago, or Minneapolis was too far outside Bob's comfort zone. Without consciously realizing it he sabotaged his opportunity and as a result didn't have to make a decision.

You don't have to be aware of the Elvis Syndrome for it to occur. In fact, the more aware you are, the more likely you can avoid it. To Bob, like other HAPs, it just seems to happen at random, almost automatically. The HAP unconsciously set the thermostat to go off. But the thermostat can be set to a higher temperature through psychotherapy, making new decisions, or other means.

> *"Success and failure are equally disastrous."*
> *— Tennessee Williams*

"Let me tell you something, big boy," Steve slurred. "I don't want to hear none of that shit from you or anyone like you. I don't have a drinking problem. You're my problem. You and Jack for sending me here. Yeah, you two assholes are my problem."

Steve was a marketing director for a midsize company when I met him. He had been extremely successful in sales, and was promoted approximately a year earlier. Jack, the company general manager, had referred Steve to me because of his concern about Steve's drinking and deteriorating performance. During a later session, Steve became less defiant but equally blunt in his commentary.

"You know why I drink?" Steve asked. "I drink because it is the only thing in my life I know I can do right. I've ruined my family, messed up my kids. I have literally destroyed everything I've ever touched. I can't even have an affair right. I'm not the man for this job. I really don't deserve it." He paused, sighed, and shrugged his shoulders slightly. "But there's one thing I can do," he continued. "I know how to drink. But I'm not an alcoholic. I drink because I want to."

Steve was in the advanced stages of the Elvis Syndrome, and the avenue he had chosen was one of low self-worth, or guilt.

Basically he had decided "I don't deserve to succeed" and was sabotaging his success by drinking. The sabotage removes the guilt by removing the success that caused it. Few people "have permission" to succeed at a high level. Permission is an unconscious process that actually results from socialization and messages received in childhood. At other times permission comes from the peer group. Some people don't feel comfortable at achieving more than their parents or peers. It's as if by out-achieving them, the group's value is diminished. Without permission or with feelings of low self-worth, self-sabotage always will occur.

In Steve's case I was unable to help him overcome his feelings of low self-worth. Twenty-three days after the discussion depicted earlier, he not only lost his job but also his freedom. While driving drunk, he was involved in a tragic accident. One person in the other car was severely injured. Another was killed. Steve is in jail. I suppose he thinks he deserves it.

"The toughest thing about success is that you've got to keep on being a success. Talent is only the starting point in this business. You've got to keep on working that talent."
—Irving Berlin

As he sat in front of me, Tom was the stereotype of what I perceived as the early sixties rock star. He could not have been easily described as black, white, or Hispanic by his appearance or language. He was dressed in typical sixties garb. Even his hollow brown eyes seemed from a different era. His music had served as anthems for me and many of my friends who served in the Vietnam War. As I sat and listened, I had difficulty separating the man I was looking at from his music. He had produced songs to which many of us had marched off to war.

"You know," he said while leaning forward. "I'm glad the music is still remembered. But that was at one point in my life. I just don't do that now. It's not what I'm about. There was a lot of money and fame. But it was more trouble than anything else. I've been in and out of drug rehab. I've known hard times. I've attempted suicide. Screwed up my life. It's been a real trip. But all most people know is the music." Tom had recorded two big hit singles and then disappeared from public view. Other than replays of his brief but powerful music, few had heard of him.

Similar to Elvis, Tom's origins were rural southern and from a low socio-economic status. His role models for handling success were all financially and vocationally unsuccessful. Still, he had excellent relationships with his parents, and other than his history of drug-related problems, he was emotionally healthy. But like many other HAPs, Tom simply had no road map of how to handle success. Tom had no experience, training, or model for handling money. He was easily taken advantage of and misdirected by shrewd business people and quickly lost all he earned. Without the education necessary to know what to do, he did a lot of things wrong.

Few people have a road map for handling success. Even fewer anticipate the difficulties, which is of course one of the major problems. As a result, there are many HAPs who experience their "fifteen minutes of fame," move on, and end up checking into Heartbreak Hotel.

> *"Experience is the fool's best teacher; the wise do not need it."*
> — *Welsh Proverb*

One of the benefits of being a psychotherapist is the opportunity to listen. I enjoy people, and I've learned a great deal simply by listening. When I visit with HAPs, I will hear about the enormous price paid by virtually all of them. I have never met a HAP who did it by coincidence or luck. The price of success is significant.

Icarus paid the ultimate price for his pursuit of success. This mythical figure decided he was going to fly to the sun. To transport himself Icarus used wax and feathers to make wings. Of course the closer he came to achieving his goal, the more quickly the wax melted. Before long he plummeted toward earth and was killed. Sometimes, achieving your goal can destroy you. This occurs occasionally because the goal itself is very destructive. By deciding to fly toward the sun, Icarus chose a goal that was literally "too hot to handle." More frequently the goal is commendable and sound. People simply underestimate the sacrifice and work required to achieve their goals. In the case of Icarus the price of success was life itself. I have seen many other examples when the price of success was marriage and family.

Topanga Jack built a small company from scratch. He began with a five-thousand-dollar loan, and several credit card cash advances. It took him thirteen years and many sleepless nights. He set up a cot in his office so he could catch catnaps rather than return home. Thirteen years after beginning his business from scratch, he netted twenty-three million dollars by selling it. What was his investment? Several thousand dollars of borrowed money. One ex-wife, who has taken him back to court over a dozen times. Three children who spent thirteen years without their father and now have nothing to do with him. As of this writing, his second marriage is deteriorating rapidly. He's an alcoholic and prescription drug addict, though he would certainly disagree with me. He has suffered from ulcers, a heart attack, and open heart surgery.

Icarus paid his price. Topanga Jack is paying his. Sometimes achieving your goal can destroy you. You need to evaluate the cost before deciding to pursue it. What price are you willing to pay?

> *"There are two tragedies in life. One is to lose your heart's desire. The other is to gain it."*
> —*George Bernard Shaw*, Men and Supermen

"You are just like your daddy. You could step in a pile of cow pies and come out smelling like a rose. If I heard it once, I've heard it a thousand times. And I'll tell you, I've gone miles out of my way to find some cow pies to jump into." A "cow pie," incidentally, is a way to describe a pile of cow dung in in the pasture.

I chuckled while listening to Cow Pies, a TV anchorman, describe his childhood. His self sabotage, both on and off camera, had made him more of a celebrity than his nightly broadcasts. It had taken us several sessions together to recognize the programming he had received from an early age. Acknowledging it was a first step in overcoming the problem.

He continued, "I probably heard him tell me I was like my daddy for the first time when I was five or six years old. At first it was my grandma I heard it from. Then my mom and my aunt. After we talked last time on the phone, I asked my mom about it. We calculate I must have been told that four or five thousand times. It's incredible.

"I mean my dad was very successful, but look what he went through. He had a severe drinking problem most of his life. He went through serious financial problems, a lot of women, a lot of grief. It was all straightened out in the end. And I guess he was considered successful. But, man alive, what he went through to get there!

"I've had a lot of the same problems he did. And I've had a lot of success. But I've taken so many detours and stepped in so many cow pies it's embarrassing. And sure, I end up smelling like a rose all right! But I told my mom, whenever we talk on the phone from now on to remind me, 'You don't have to step in a pile of cow pies to end up smelling like a rose. You can skip the cow pies—there's an easier way!'"

Cow Pies' story is too familiar. His family had no intention of sending the negative message that going through piles was the way to success, nor did they attempt to create negative programming. After all, his father had been an incredibly successful military officer and pilot. The comparison was actually made as a compliment. And the resulting success spoke for itself. However, the steps it took him to get there resulted in substantial and unnecessary pain. Becoming aware of the problem and taking steps to overcome it helped him avoid the pain—the 'piles'—in his future.

"Forget your personal tragedy. We are all bitched from the start, and you especially have to hurt like hell before you can write seriously. But when you get the damn hurt, use it—don't cheat with it."
—Ernest Hemingway in a letter to F. Scott Fitzgerald

Tammy had been one of the most creative people I had ever met. She was a copywriter for an advertising agency by trade and an artist with tremendous painting talent by passion. Her hobby was playing cello with the local symphony orchestra when she wasn't singing with a small country band. I had met her years ago when I was the keynote speaker at a convention she attended. We stayed in touch with each other for a few years and finally drifted apart.

The next time I heard from her was when she called for professional help. She had quit her job, had an affair, and ultimately moved out of town with her boyfriend. She eventually grew quite depressed and became addicted to drugs. A suicide attempt followed the drug dependency. When it failed she developed an eating disorder. Her boy friend ultimately kicked her out, and she had moved back home. By the time I met with her she was in immense difficulty.

This phenomenon happens to creative people far more frequently than to the rest of the population. Creativity and destructiveness are opposite sides of the same coin. Creative energy unexpressed will become destructive energy, and is almost always directed inward. The negative emotion is introjected instead of projected. Like many highly creative people who have no outlet for their energy, Tammy became self-destructive. She was not only cannibalizing her talent but her very life as well. Her recovery was complicated and painstakingly slow. Yet the more she expressed her creativity, the healthier she became.

There are people who simply must create. If they don't, their tremendous creative energy will be expressed self-destructively. Often the result will be suicide, first symbolically and then literally. Creativity and destructiveness always go together. The intensity of one is matched by the other. This avenue is one of the speedways leading to Heartbreak Hotel. It's also probably the primary path Elvis used.

"Sic transit gloria mundae." (So passes away the glory of this world.)
— *Thomas A. Kinder,* The Imitation of Christ

The Roman tradition, mentioned in Chapter One, certainly prevented various heroes of the day from believing their own press clippings—such as there were back then. Unfortunately, modern society is void of any formal equivalent. A staff member riding in the President's limousine, reminding him of his mortality or calling him a bald adulterer, would obviously be unwelcome. Stand-up comedians and actors on *Saturday Night Live* may serve a similar function, but the President unfortunately doesn't have to watch. Apparently President Bush, during his administration, watched himself being parodied by Saturday Night Live veteran Dana Carvey. Perhaps it helped him keep perspective. Roman conquerors didn't self-destruct from a swelled head infected by media overexposure. However, countless thousands of others since that day probably have.

Unfortunately, some people become extremely deluded with their infected and swollen head. They can become not only self-destructive but dangerous to others as well. O.J. Simpson is a recent example. There are examples, however, that had far more deadly consequences. David Koresh and Jim Jones demonstrated to the world what can occur when people begin to consider themselves part of the deity. The danger of this process is historically underestimated. Being idolized and worshiped result in people feeling worthy of being worshiped. It is very unnatural.

As this occurs people begin to feel godlike. This is the critical point where they begin to feel normal rules don't apply to them, and simple cause and effect relationships don't either. This is probably one reason HAPs in the spotlight experience so many drug overdoses. They feel invincible, bulletproof, and that normal rules don't apply. After all, they're being worshiped, idolized, and adored. From Vincent Van Gogh to F. Scott Fitzgerald to John Candy, experience has taught us one thing. Normal rules apply to everyone. And, as Michael Milken, Jim Bakker, and Leona Helmsly can tell you, the laws apply as well. This is such a significant part of the Elvis Syndrome it is discussed in detail later.

"Being willing to suffer in order to create is one thing; to realize that sort of creation necessitates one's suffering, that suffering is one of the greatest of God's gifts, is almost to reach a mystical solution to the puzzle of evil ."
—J. W. N. Sullivan

The next time I heard from Curtis was several months later, in August. Sorting through the mail, I noticed his scribbling on an envelope. Other than the zip code, it was almost illegible. I chuckled while opening it. Inside was a greeting card. It was a picture of a young Elvis from the 1950's. Inside the envelope he had included a personal letter. On the card he had written the words "Dr. B.—Happy dead Elvis week."

I laughed and turned to Bud, who works with me. "What's dead Elvis week?" I asked

"Oh, it's a big deal in Memphis," he responded. "People come from all over. It's the anniversary of his death—August 16th. They do it up the whole week. It's a big event. What's that you got there anyway?"

I handed Bud the card while opening the personal letter. Curtis initially updated me on his daughter's progress in college and discussed some other family news. I read the letter quickly but was surprised by the last paragraph.

"I think you need to go ahead and do something with this idea about self-destructiveness. I actually think our entire country is doing it. Obviously it's happening in the current administration, but it's bigger than that. I really believe the whole country is flushing itself down the commode.

"America is going through the same stages as Elvis did. We started off poor and humble. So did he. Then we became successful—a "world power." So did he. Since then we've become bloated, deluded, and drugged by our excesses. So did he. I really believe the whole damn country is self-destructing. Elvis self-destructed. I know there's a difference between an entire country and one person, but I simply believe our country is self-destructing. The question is how do we stop it before it's too late? There's not room enough for the whole country in Heartbreak Hotel! But we're all heading there . . . ."

That night I couldn't sleep. I woke up at 2:30 a.m. and began writing.

SUMMARY

"Typical" Evolution of a HAP
Stage One—education and preparation.
Stage Two—early skill refinement.
Stage Three—intense training and skill refinement.
Stage Four—initial success which leads to three choices:
  • level out and grow comfortable with current success level
  • enter lower stages of the Elvis Syndrome or diversify into other areas.
  • enter stage five of the Elvis Syndrome.
Stage Five—exponential success.
Stage Six—death by success.

JOURNAL SESSION

1. Refer to the "Typical Evolution of a HAP" from the previous page. It might be interesting to chart your own career development by discussing what you did at each stage. As an example: Stage One—went to high school and college; bachelor's degree in accounting. Stage Two—job paying low wages in accounting department of insurance company. Stage Three—night school while continuing career. Stage Four—promoted to department head. Comfortable with position; still there today, etc.

2. Discuss what you perceive as *success*. Discuss what you perceive as *happiness* and how you would measure it. Define whether the two are similar. Discuss whether achieving success will "make" you happier than you are today.

3. The *success thermostat* and *comfort zone* concepts are difficult for most people to understand. As an example, few believe they actually control their own thermostat and sometimes self-sabotage to keep from succeeding outside of its limits. Discuss in writing what you define as your success comfort zone. If you were promoted to your boss's job tomorrow, would you feel comfortable? Look for times in your life when you have suc-

ceeded beyond that level and then unconsciously created difficulties that brought you back within your comfort zone.

4. Your parents may or may not have been effective role models, especially when it came to dealing with success. If they were, you are lucky. If they weren't, it is important to identify someone who could serve as a role model for you. If it's someone with whom you could have a mentor relationship, that would be ideal. Choose someone you can study or read about who has lived the kind of life you would like to emulate.

CHECKLIST

Directions: Rate each trait below on a scale from zero (does not apply to me at all) to five (applies a great deal of the time).

___1. I measure success by the three "R's"—respect, recognition and remuneration.

___2. In my opinion rich people are by far more happy than those who aren't rich.

___3. My heroes are people who would be considered wealthy.

___4. In my opinion success is happiness and happiness is success.

___5. In my opinion happiness is something you can achieve.

___6. I would be much happier if I had more money.

___7. To me, winning in competition is highly important. I don't consider a game worth playing if I don't have a chance to win.

___8. I consider myself someone who has internalized society's expectations.

___9. In all honesty I probably have poor role models for handling success.

___10. The childhood programming I received probably prepared me more for failure than success.

___11. If I don't set exceptionally high standards on a personal level, I will probably end up inferior.

___12. If I make a mistake, I'm convinced people will think less of me.

___13. If I can't excel at something or at least do it extremely well, I'm better off not doing it at all.

___14. If I make a mistake, I should be upset at myself or punish myself.

___15. If I really try hard, I should be able to excel at anything.

___16. It is bad or shameful for me to display a weakness or be involved in frivolous or non-serious behavior.

___17. I should never repeat a mistake.

___18. An average or mediocre performance is never satisfying.

___19. I am much less of a person if I fail at something important.

___20. It will help me improve if I am hard on myself for not doing as well as I could.

___Total

How to Score Yourself: Total your score. If it is less than twenty-five, your risk for the Elvis Syndrome is probably low. Totals from twenty-five through fifty indicate beginning stages of the Elvis Syndrome. Fifty through seventy-five suggest problematic behavior that probably is hindering achievement and relationships. Scores over seventy-five suggest a need for caution. It would be helpful for you to discuss this questionnaire with a professional.

Chapter 3

CAUGHT IN THE TRAP
SYMPTOMS OF DEATH BY SUCCESS

"There is no great genius without some touch of madness."
— Seneca from De Tranquillitate Animi

To understand how Elvis's reign as king ended, you must first look at his beginning. The two-room shotgun shack of what was then called Old Saltillo Road is still there. They were called shotgun shacks because you could stand in the front door and shoot a shotgun out the back door. Elvis Aaron Presley was born January 8, 1935, in Tupelo, Mississippi. The city's population at the time was six thousand. His identical twin brother, Jesse Garen, was stillborn. This resulted in what most people have described as an overprotective attitude by his mother, Gladys, which persisted to her premature death on August 14, 1958.

It was the Great Depression and times were difficult. His father, Vernon, spent some time in jail during Elvis's childhood for altering a check. Some suggest this resulted in Gladys and Elvis becoming even closer. His life in Tupelo centered around his mother and the First Assembly of God Church. Elvis once described his dancing style as originating in this small church. "We used to go to these religious services all the time. There were these singers, perfectly fine singers, but nobody responded to them. Then there was the preachers, and they cut up all over the place, jumping on the piano and moving every which-a-way. I guess I learned from them."

Vernon Presley moved his family to Memphis, where he found work in 1948 as a truck driver. Gladys got a job as a sewing machine operator. By this time Elvis had gotten his first guitar and was singing in the church choir. He was already beginning to develop talent, but the move to Memphis would prove vital to his career. He was a quiet, shy, reserved teenager who let his personality express itself only during talent shows, which he won. Elvis had problems with sleepwalking. He was so embarrassed and frightened by it, that he slept with his parents until early adulthood. This was tolerated probably because his mother feared something terrible would happen, as it had to his twin brother.

But just as the move to Memphis was prophetic, so was his relationship with Gladys. His career actually began as a result of this relationship. After graduating from high school, Elvis got a job driving a truck for Crown Electric in Memphis, for thirty-five dollars a week. In the summer of 1953, he paid Sun Record Studios four dollars to record a couple of songs for his mother. Marion Keisker, a secretary, liked Elvis's voice and kept a tape of the session. Eight months later, Sun's president, Sam Phillips was looking for someone who could be a "black sound inside a white body."

"What about the kid with sideburns?" Marion asked. Sam listened to the tape, talked to Elvis, and took four months to call him back. In August 1954, *That's All Right, Mama* was released. It had been one year since he had recorded the four-dollar present for his mother, and five years since moving to Memphis. Needless to say, there were no recording studios at the time in Tupelo, and definitely no agents for Sun Records. This was the true beginning of the Elvis phenomenon.

Elvis Presley was a product of his socialization. He was terminally shy, fanatically devoted to his mother, and sincerely respectful of authority. He was of deprived origins and a fundamental religious family. In Tupelo during the Depression, race relations were quite harmonious. Poor whites shared intimately the lives of poor blacks, with whom they probably had more in common than other whites. And Elvis, like many others of his culture, had tremendous exposure to black gospel, rhythm and blues, and country music as well. But most all of his exposure was two hundred-proof southern. And it was all vital not only to his success, but also to his premature death.

Elvis was a southern fried phenomenon in the summer of 1953. His deferential manner toward authority and his shy, country boy attitude were part of the attraction. Elvis never changed. The eleven-year-old who jump-started a local talent show. The eighteen-year-old who laid down four dollars to record his mother's songs. The low lids, curled lip, and a voice that could stretch an unbelievable range of emotions out of one word. The sensual, wild movements he copied from watching Assembly of God preachers. It was all Elvis until his death. He was simple and complex hated confrontation, and wanted to please everyone; humble and profane; rough-edged and smooth-voiced. Elvis was a living contradiction. He changed the course of American music, and he changed the course of America.

"A man in a passion rides a horse that runs away with him."
— Thomas Ford

Death by success. The concept itself is a paradox. But it happened to Elvis. And it could be happening to you. In fact, it probably is happening to you or to someone you know. It happens to superstars but also to people from all imaginable walks of life. You don't have to succeed in mammoth proportions to experience the Elvis Syndrome. The symptoms can occur with the smallest level of achievement and appear in various stages. The Elvis Syndrome is a progressive phenomenon that can be measured methodically.

Achievement is, in fact, the first and most comprehensive symptom. It's relative and can include being promoted simply from minimum wage to twenty-five cents an hour above minimum. Yet achievement alone doesn't cause the Elvis Syndrome. Personality style also plays an important role. The classically defined Type A personality is the one most vulnerable to death by success.

The Type A pattern is most clearly recognized by its combination of risk, impatience, and competition. These people are often described as harried, hurried, and hostile. Type A people are usually punctual, organized, and goal-oriented. They resemble people you already know. Perhaps you are a Type A. One study indicated they may account for sixty percent of the population. Generally, they strive, and striving appears to be the key. They strive to accomplish too much, participate in too many activities, and stuff more into less time. They create unnecessary deadlines, hurry chronically, and compete at everything. They avoid standing in line at all costs, do at least two or three things simultaneously, and resultingly suffer many health problems, such as ulcers, headaches, and high blood pressure. Many typical fast-paced achievers in today's society would probably fall into this category.

As a result of the striving mentioned above, various things occur. Type A people develop an aggressive drive, often developing into chronic hostility. Because of their work habits they usually develop few hobbies. The hobbies they do develop become part of the problem because Type A's turn all things into competition. They have no diversions and feel guilty relaxing. Due to this tension buildup, Type A's experiment with short-term attempts to escape. Usually this will result in alcohol or other drug addiction. They also often over-eat and smoke more than others.

Type A's have tremendous difficulty with *control*. They have a need to control others bordering on the bizarre. As a result it is almost impossible for them to delegate responsibility, or get along with others. Most Type A's will have few relationships other than those at work, and most of those are unsatisfying due to their high need for control. They become lonely, and unhappy, so they work harder. The cycle repeats itself with increasing intensity.

Type A's are three times more likely to suffer coronary risks than the rest of the population. Nearly all Type A's will at some time experience severe health problems mentioned above. Hostility and anger appear to be the main culprits leading to those maladies. Usually the rage is triggered by another person. In fact, in isolation from others, some Type A's seem to function quite well. Mixed with others—even in a marriage, however— the Type A can become combustible.

This behavior is typical of most stage one HAPs. However, other factors must be present for Type A's to become Elvis

Syndrome victims. There are a variety of these, beginning with brazen risk taking. The stage one HAP getting caught in the trap flirts with danger tempestuously. These risks are taken with career, money, and their body. It's as if the rush from such things creates an almost drugged effect. The risks are also unnecessary. It's risk taking for its own sake. They ultimately live on the edge, always on the brink of disaster. Eventually this high-risk behavior results in being cut off from others and eventually isolated. Stage one HAPs trust nobody. They become suspicious and even paranoid of family, friends, and associates. As HAPs become more successful, the distrust grows more pervasive. Everyone is suspected. Fears that others like them only because of their success or money consume the stage one HAPs. At this point they often divorce or change friends, increasing the isolation.

> *"Men must have corrupted nature a little for they were not born wolves,*
> *and they have become wolves."*
> *— Voltaire*

There are stories of Elvis experimenting sexually over the twenty-odd years of his stardom. Obviously, women were attracted to him. Toward the end there were reports of sexual impotence, but the king was always accompanied by women. Some say he used women as an escape—to ease the pain. Elvis didn't enjoy being alone, and perhaps the women were mere companions. In fact, it was his fiancée, Ginger Alden, who discovered Elvis lying on the floor on the day of his death. Yet at the same time he was engaged to Ginger, he was apparently courting several other women. Toward the end he even attempted a brief fling with a fifteen-year-old.

Sexual experimentation is common among stage two HAPs. Sometimes this experimentation includes promiscuity, prostitution, and at times homosexual activity. Stage two HAPs have no fear of AIDS or other sexual disease. They consider themselves above such dangers. In fact, during stage two they can develop such feelings of grandiosity that they become quite arrogant not only in sexual relationships but in all aspects of their lives. Their stance becomes defiant and at times delusional. Leona Helmsley's claim that "only little people pay taxes" is an illustration of this.

This kind of thinking leads to greed. Occasionally the greed is directed toward things or money, but the most frequent manifestation of greed is toward success itself. Stage two HAPs simply can't achieve enough. They feel like it's never good enough. This ultimately leads to a combination of guilt, shame, and anxiety that can become toxic. As a result they often work harder to mask those feelings and eventually become workaholics. At this point they're not working to achieve, but to hide feelings. As long as they're working, they don't have to worry about what's bothering them.

Stage-two HAPs also begin a process of personal insulation. This is a reciprocal process involving both the HAP and those around him or her. Insulation goes beyond distrust. At this point they will associate only with like-minded individuals who not only avoid disagreeing but prevent others from doing the same. Elvis, as an example, was accompanied by his "Memphis Mafia," bodyguards, aides, and groupies. They seemed obsessed with insulating him from other people and, in some cases, even from other information. They helped, fed, and even medicated Elvis. Mike Tyson had a similar entourage with similar results. So did Michael Jackson. And O.J. And Tonya Harding. And on and on and on. Clearly such isolation is a serious problem. It's not only a symptom of the Elvis Syndrome but a contributing cause as well.

> *"Fame is a powerful aphrodisiac."*
> *— Graham Greene*

There have been various reports of Elvis's fascination with police badges. At one time he collected them, but it appears Elvis took this hobby one step further. As discussed earlier, Elvis was quite respectful of authority. His "Yes, Ma'ams" and "No, Ma'ams" came from deep within his southern soul. Most HAPs are equally compliant. In Chapter Two we found the typical HAP accepts the "rules" and then works very hard within the framework they provide. Elvis never would have considered dodging the draft. When he got drafted he served his time and ended up with the *GI Blues*. Most HAPs do the same. They work within the rules, though perhaps occasionally pushing the limits.

An example of this is found in their attitude toward drugs. HAPs often experience intense levels of compulsions and addictions. Usually all who advance to stage three struggle with this. In most, it begins with alcohol. Some celebrated HAPs also have problems with illegal drugs. But due to their authoritative nature, the culprit is far more likely to be legal. At a minimum their drug of choice will be socially acceptable. Elvis was addicted to drugs. To him, however, he wasn't a drug addict. They were all prescribed, usually by his physician, Dr. George Nichopoulos. Occasionally they were prescribed by others, including dentists. Like many other HAPs, there was apparently a distinction in his mind. Since they were legal and prescribed by a major authority figure (a physician), they were okay. I've been told by HAPs dozens of times "I don't use drugs. They're legal medicine. I've got a prescription for them. This isn't a drug. Heroin is a drug."

Elvis reportedly feared street drugs and usually avoided them. In December 1970 he visited the Nixon White House and apparently engaged in discussions about drug problems within the music industry. Elvis was reportedly armed during the visit and even wore his signature white cape. Elvis gave Nixon a commemorative pistol and Nixon gave Elvis a Federal Narcotics Bureau badge. Elvis was supposed to, in turn, keep Nixon informed on illegal drug activity among entertainers. While some people look at this comically, both addiction and denial are actual tragic symptoms of the Elvis Syndrome. Elvis denied he had drug problems, because he had prescriptions. Alcohol is a drug. Heroin, cocaine, and marijuana are drugs. Mind-altering prescription medications are also drugs. Denying it does not change it. Jaded denial only makes it worse. If you refuse to face the problem, you can never solve it. These factors are such major parts of the Elvis Syndrome that an entire chapter is devoted to them later.

Most stage three HAPs will also experience compulsive problems other than alcoholism or drug addiction. These compulsions can extend to gambling, sex, pornography, eating, and, as mentioned earlier, work. The term *compulsion* is used here to describe *any powerful behavior or habit repeated on a regular basis with potential negative consequences.* The difference between a simple habit and a compulsion sometimes appears to be thin. Compulsions, however, seem to take on a power of their own. The HAP feels compelled to participate in the habit. Compulsions are also more ritualized, including occasional idiosyncratic patterns. Handwashing, as an example, is a desirable habit, but washing your hands two hundred times a day and not letting it count unless it involves ritualistic movements of the hands is a compulsion. In the same way, spending an hour on a slot machine once every two or three years when you go to Las Vegas is gambling. Borrowing money to bet on a ball game when you are two months behind on your house payment, however, is evidence of compulsion. Having sexual intercourse with your spouse several times a week is healthy. Missing work so you can have sex the fourth time that day is a compulsion. I have worked with stage three HAPs in therapy experiencing each of these compulsions.

The compulsions often take on a visceral quality. Frequently HAPs will exhibit a near-frenetic level of kinetic activity, appearing to be tics, twitches, or just nervous habits. Appearing to be maniacally hyper, they just can't seem to stay still. These tendencies often lead to mistaken assumptions by observers that the HAP is on cocaine. Most HAPs don't have to use cocaine. They are often on a perpetual adrenaline rush. Rapidly chewing gum, rhythmically bobbing their heads, or anxiously tapping their feet, HAPs constantly give the appearance of a first-graders in need of Ritalin. And the most incredible thing of all is the total lack of awareness of it all. They are oblivious to their lives and careers tumbling down around them.

"The vanity of others runs counter to our taste only when it runs counter to our vanity."
—*Friederick Nietzsche*, Beyond Good and Evil

If you review this chapter thus far, you will notice the Elvis Syndrome is very methodical. The symptoms worsen over time and become increasingly chronic. During stage four development, the severity of problems mushroom ominously. It's at this point HAPs figuratively and literally begin losing contact with reality. The first sign of this is a minimization of guilt and loss of conscience. This can be a devastating development and is one of the most severe symptoms in the entire syndrome. If a HAP advances to stage four, he or she is irreversibly caught in the trap.

Many years ago Sigmund Freud hypothesized a personality structure including what he called the ego, superego, and id. The ego served to cope with everyday reality by thinking, mediating, and balancing other parts of the personality. Since then, ego has come to describe someone with an inflated opinion of himself. But that was not part of Freud's original theory. The ego operates on what Freud called the *reality principle*. The id, on the other hand, was driven by what Freud called the *pleasure principle*. He described it as a storehouse of unconscious impulses. Selfishness, rage, and aggressive tendencies all originated in the id. An unbridled id could not only be dangerous but homicidal according to Freud. To prevent such danger, the ego drew from what Freud called the superego. The superego includes what we call the conscience. It helps us distinguish between right and wrong. It is responsible for impulse control and prevents us from acting out or expressing violent urges. Freud would say self-control and guilt result from superego activity. Too much or not enough guilt or control would be caused by unhealthy or inadequate superego development. However you define this process, it is clearly an important one. Conscience is also one of the first areas where the advanced-level HAP loses control. Stage four HAPs initially experience a minimization of conscience and guilt. Often this is the beginning of the end.

There are people who either never developed a conscience or have lost contact with it. Lack of guilt or conscience can result in a person becoming very dangerous—usually to others. Too much guilt, on the other hand, can be dangerous as well. It can inhibit a person as severely as any illness. Without guilt there is literally nothing to prevent someone from hurting others. And with too much guilt the individual hurts himself.

With the loss of conscience, the stage four HAP can develop what is commonly called *sociopathic* tendencies. Sociopaths constitute a large part of the criminal population. Most institutionalized criminals probably could be diagnosed with this problem. People with this disorder can be very dangerous to others. A true sociopath doesn't blink. He or she has little or no conscience, and therefore has no guilt. His or her heart rate and blood pressure may actually lower when committing an act of violence, whether it's physical or emotional. One reason these people feel so calm is that they hold nothing back and therefore are allowed to focus exclusively on their own pleasure.

As a result, stage four HAPs develop a narcissistic attitude. They become overwhelmingly self-absorbed and self-centered. Whether others are inconvenienced or injured is irrelevant. The narcissistic individual usually spends excessive time on self and is overly concerned with appearances. How things appear to the stage four HAP is far more important than how things really are. They obsess on the superficial and ignore reality. This marked self-centeredness and lack of conscience allow the stage four HAPs to become obsessed. And usually they become obsessed with success at any cost and preoccupied with themselves. They begin to ponder their own plight narcissistically. This usually results in a preoccupation with self and ultimately a preoccupation with their own life and death.

Elvis developed this toward the end of his life. He was obsessed with his deteriorating physical appearance, deeply troubled by the soon-to-be-released book written by two former bodyguards and preoccupied with his own death. There are reports he staged midnight visits to the Memphis morgue where he conducted rambling monologues on the subject of death. When his fiancée's aunt died, he hinted to friends he would join her soon. In the last days, it was as if he was making peace and preparing to die. I believe the King was deeply depressed and had decided at this point to take his life. He simply was awaiting the right time.

"The mass of men lead lives of quiet desperation. What is called resignation is confirmed desperation. A stereotyped but unconscious despair is concealed even under what are called the games and amusements of mankind."
— Thoreau

Depression is the common cold of emotional problems. Everybody experiences it to one degree or another, at some point in his or her life. You can get depressed because your team loses the ball game, but that's more like discouragement. The depression we find at stages five and six is pure despair. And usually, in initial phases, it manifests itself quietly. This is serious depression, which involves the most severe kind of emotional introjection. At this point, most negative emotions are turned inward. People experiencing such depression talk about feeling swallowed up, the walls closing in, and being consumed by the pain. They describe a black cloud and a feeling of impending doom wherever they go. At times deeply depressed people can even appear dead. Emotional and physical rigor mortis appears to set in. The ultimate form of this kind of depression is death. Sometimes it is a dramatic suicide. At other times it's slower, progressing one miserable inch at a time. But the result is the same.

Occasionally the depression is masked by what appears to be uncontrollable rage and outbursts of intense anger. Some describe the stage five HAP as a rage-aholic with episodes of sadistic, ruthless and even brutal behavior toward others. Regardless of position, power or influence, a series of troubled relationships soon follows. This includes an inability to make emotional commitments and usually a series of affairs or shallow sexual relationships. This is all, however, a part of the depression. Usually the depression begins due to external circumstances. The HAP is usually responding to disappointment, emptiness, or troubled relationships he or she is experiencing. At some point the depression can change and become a condition more internally based. Few people clearly understand the seriousness of this sort of biochemical depression. One HAP described it "as if a switch had been flipped inside his head somewhere." This sort of depression is more than exaggerated sadness and can be fatal. At one extreme it can lead to absolute giving up and suicide. At a minimum it results in the person becoming even more self-absorbed, concerned about her own pains and pleasures, and further isolated from others and reality as well.

"The human being as a commodity is the disease of our age."
—Max Lerner

Stage six HAPs have progressively lost more and more contact with reality. At this point they use people as objects and objects as people. People are used as a means to an end. When the HAP enters a relationship, it's only to boost his or her own career or status. The HAP's emotional attachments turn toward objects. They surround themselves with, and become very attached to things. Money, jewelry, cars, and clothing take on more meaning than friends or family. Even in a crowd they look lonely, though in reality they are rarely actually alone. Yet the void exists. To fill the void they develop a win-at-all-costs attitude and usually direct it toward one particular goal. They becomes fixated. Sometimes the fixation is with career. Other times it's with people. Regardless of the fixated object, the win-at-all-costs attitude is directed with laser focus. And woe to the object of that focus, especially if it's another person.

Elvis, from the early years to death, was fixated with his career. The year after releasing *That's All Right, Mama*, Elvis, Scotty Moore, and Bill Black went on tour. They drove a forty-five-hundred-mile loop beginning and ending in Memphis, staging more than two hundred twenty one-night stands. In Biloxi, Mississippi, they performed for the dedication of a fraternal hall's new air conditioner. Their fee? Supper. During his brief life and even shorter career, he made thirty-three movies. Not a single one lost money. At one point the merchandising of Elvis rivaled even the campaigns of today's ad agency icons. There were, of course, the typical Elvis records and movies. There were Elvis photographs, posters, T-shirts, sweatshirts, ball cards, and caps. Then it began to stretch. There were Elvis shoes, socks, shirts, and shorts. There was an Elvis belt to wear on your Elvis jeans, and an Elvis Presley handkerchief so you could wipe your nose before going to sleep in your Elvis Presley pajamas. If the list of Elvis Presley paraphernalia made you tired, you could refresh yourself with an Elvis Presley soft drink. The people who designed and manufactured this merchandise were marketing people, not Elvis. Primarily this paraphernalia was a result of the industrious Colonel Tom Parker, Elvis's business manager. Yet Elvis received a ten- to fifteen-percent commission on each item. Due to the nature of the relationship, it is sometimes difficult to delineate Elvis's tendencies from the Colonel's. But regardless, because of the Colonel or on his own, Elvis was laser focused, to the point that it became more of a problem than an asset.

"The charm of fame is so great that we like every object to which it is attached, even death."
—Blaise Pascal

By the end of his life, Elvis had zeroed out on his ability to cope. He reacted to his obesity with shame and embarrassment. He never seemed to recover from his mother's death. His drug problems had become unmanageable. He was reported to be sexually impotent. There were some reports that due to mismanagement, his financial empire was about to collapse. One reporter even predicted an impending bankruptcy and suggested only Elvis's death could have changed that. Paradoxically, the same reporter suggested accurately Elvis would be worth far more dead than living.

Someone else suggested it was Elvis's inability to cope with an exposé—published by former bodyguards, Sammy and Red West—that precipitated his suicide. Such explanations are unfair to the bodyguards. It actually was his zero ability to cope. If it wasn't their book, it would have been something else. In reality, the Wests seem to have been very devoted to Elvis. Those who claim their book put him over the edge simply don't understand. Elvis's inability to cope, not the book, created the problem.

Elvis's life also illustrates one of the final symptoms of death by success. In virtually all cases, stage six HAPs reflect a childhood either filled with inadequate relationships or an otherwise troubled past. There is no evidence Elvis suffered any kind of abuse or neglect. His father, as mentioned earlier, was absent for a period of time due to incarceration. There have been other suggestions that Vernon was generally psychologically unavailable, especially during Elvis's childhood. But his mother, Gladys, doted on Elvis and acted as if he could do no wrong. This combination, an enmeshed-and-doting mother and psychologically absent father, seems to be the most prevalent parenting pattern found with HAPs experiencing death by success. Unfortunately, however, it's usually realized and investigated only in retrospect. This phenomenon is discussed further in another chapter.

> *"Fame has also this great drawback, that if we pursue it we must direct our lives in such a way as to please the fancy of men, avoiding what they dislike and seeking what is pleasing to them."*
> *—Baruch Spinoza (1632-1677)*

From the shotgun shack to Graceland, Elvis's life personified the American dream. He touched America and changed the course of history. Whether his death was suicide or accidental is irrelevant. Either way, his early death was unnecessary. He died at age forty-two—approximately the same age as Roseanne Barr, Robin Williams, and Hulk Hogan were at the time this book was published. On January 8, 1995, Elvis would have turned sixty. He would have been younger than Clint Eastwood or *Bewitched* star Elizabeth Montgomery, and approximately the same age as Woody Allen and Richard Chamberlain. He would have been only two years older than Robert Redford, Warren Beatty, and Dustin Hoffman—all still leading men today. He would have been far younger than Mike Wallace, Dan Rather, or Paul Newman. He would have been approximately three years older than Jane Fonda, and three years younger than Barbara Walters. In other words, he still would have been considered young by today's standards. But he's dead.

At the time of his autopsy Elvis had *ten times* the fatal level of codeine in his body. In addition he had ingested the following, all taken in the twenty-four hours before he died:

Amytal—muscle relaxant	*Nembutal*—barbituate
Aventyl—antidepressant	*Quaalude*—narcotic sleeping pill
Carbrital—sleeping pill	*Sinutab*—antihistamine and
Valmid—insomnia tranquilizer	decongestant
Demerol—narcotic analgesic	*Valium*—tranquilizer
Elavil—antidepressant	*morphine*—narcotic pain reliever

All but the Sinutab were prescribed medication. It was the perfect prescription for death.

JOURNAL SESSION

1. As mentioned in the chapter, many successful people have Type A personalities. This can be good or bad depending on the circumstances. Being punctual is generally considered to be good, but there are some people who refuse to be late. Knowing they'll be late to an appointment, they will either cancel or not show up at all. Discuss the times you've done this. Discuss in writing times when you have taken other "good" qualities to such an extreme.

2. Describe your hobbies. Separate those that are competitive and those that are not. Discuss whether or not you would engage in the competitive hobbies you've chosen if you were not able to win or compete.

3. Make a list of your closest friends, outside of spouse or family. Beside their names, write the date you first met them. Describe the last time you spoke to them. Have any of them known you more than five years? Why or why not?

4. Examine your life closely for compulsions. Discuss whether alcohol, drugs, sex, gambling, or eating (to name a few) are causing problems in your career and relationships. Discuss the compulsions your parents experienced and whether or not they are the same for you.

5. List your closest friends. Beside their names note who is related to you and who are your employees. Can *you* be totally honest with *anyone*? Choose two names and discuss why it is or is not possible for you to be honest with them. Discuss whether there is anyone on the list you can be honest with.

HAP Alphabet Stage Indicator

Stage One
A = Achievement-oriented personality
B = Brazen, risk taking
C = Cut off from others
D = Distrust of family, friends and associates

Stage Two
E = Experimentation, sexual and otherwise
F = Feelings of grandiosity and arrogance
G = Greed of an unusual nature
H = High level of depression

Stage Three
I = Intense addiction and compulsions
J = Jaded sense of denial
K = Kinetic activity—high level kinetic activity
L = Lack of conscience and guilt

Stage Four
M = Minimal awareness and minimization
N = Narcissism
O = Obsessing with achievement and proving competence
P = Preoccupation with career

Stage Five
Q = Quiet desperation
R = Rage-aholic
S = Sadistic and ruthless behavior toward others
T = Troubled relationships and ability to keep commitments

Stage Six
U = Uses people as objects and objects as people
V = Very preoccupied with material things
W = Win-at-all-costs attitude
X = X-ray focus and narrow vision

Contributing factors:
Y = Youth filled with inadequate parenting
Z = Zero ability to cope

CHECKLIST

Directions: Check each one that applies to you.

Stage One

___1. Being punctual is extremely important to me. If I know I am going to be late, I will sometimes cancel altogether.

___2. I often feel that I have too many things to do and not enough time for them.

___3. I find it difficult to delegate tasks to others. I feel it's usually easier to do it myself and have it done right the first time.

___4. I have few friends other than those with whom I work.

___5. I experience angry outbursts that seem to surface for no reason.

___6. I feel driven to achieve.

___7. I feel that if something is worth doing, it is worth doing right or not at all.

___8. I have difficulty trusting other people, even on the job.

___9. On many occasions I have sped in my car far too fast for road conditions.

___10. I don't feel I have time for hobbies. It's necessary for me to spend as much time as I can on my job.

___ Total for Stage One.

Stage Two

___1. I have engaged in "sexually promiscuous behavior."

___2. I have experimented with homosexual behavior.

___3. I have engaged in sexual behavior as if there were no such thing as AIDS.

___4. I'm often afraid my success won't last.

___5. People who disagree with me just don't understand me.

___6. I don't allow others who have negative outlooks on my life or mission to be around me.

_____7. I've earned the right to be successful. I've followed the rules and paid my dues.

_____8. I know I'm on the right track because those closest to me agree with my point of view.

_____9. I fear that most people like me only because I'm successful. They want favors or money from me.

_____10. I have one or two close associates without whom I wouldn't make any decisions.

_____ Total for Stage Two.

Stage Three

_____1. I believe in authority and submit myself to those whom I consider my superiors.

_____2. Friends have told me I need to drink less.

_____3. Alcohol or drugs have created problems for me.

_____4. My parents have or have had problems with drugs.

_____5. I have been told I am "hyper." Others have accused me of being on drugs.

_____6. Most of the people whom I consider my friends are my employees too.

_____7. I don't have a drug problem since everything I take is prescribed by a doctor.

_____8. I often feel that most people are too critical of me.

_____9. I sometimes have to take unusual measures to protect myself from jealous people.

_____10. I am more than fifteen pounds overweight.

_____ Total for Stage Three.

Stage Four

_____1. I have few if any outside interests or hobbies except those related to my career.

_____2. To remain successful, I must consistently improve what I am doing.

_____3. I feel my spouse and/or family doesn't understand or appreciate my dedication to my career.

_____4. My family often nags me to do activities and to go places with them. To get where I want to be, I cannot take leave of my job for that long.

___5. I find it almost impossible to sit still. I need to be doing something at all times.

___6. I have used sleeping pills or alcohol to help me relax.

___7. Friends or family have told me I have an (alcohol, gambling, drug, etc.) problem, but I know I'm not an addict.

___8. When I do have to stay in one place for a long time (e.g. in an airplane or meeting), a part of my body remains in motion. I will chew gum, swing my leg, or my arms might twitch.

___9. Without question, my career is the most important thing in my life.

___10. People have accused me of being too absorbed in my own life.

___ Total for Stage Four.

Stage Five

___1. I get depressed often.

___2. There have been times when I was so depressed or upset that I didn't care whether I lived or died.

___3. I have seriously thought about suicide, or wished more than once that I would simply die.

___4. Anger is a serious problem for me.

___5. I sometimes have fits of rage.

___6. I have thrown things, broken things, or hit people or objects in anger.

___7. There are times in my life when I have been very cruel to others.

___8. I have purposely injured an animal more than once.

___9. I've experienced one or more divorces.

___10. I have difficulty maintaining long-term relationships.

___ Total for Stage Five.

Stage Six

___1. I consider people generally undependable.

___2. It's easier to depend on my car than someone else.

___3. The honest truth is, I'm more attached to my (jewelry, car, horse, boat, etc.) than I am to other people.

___4. It's important to me to wear name-brand clothes.

___5. The type of car a person drives says a lot about his or her personality.

___6. The neighborhood you live in can determine a great deal of your status.

___7. My reputation is important to my career. I'm only as good as my last song, or business deal, or speech, etc.

___8. My motto is "Winning Is What Matters."

___9. I sometimes get so focused on my goals that I forget about other people.

___10. At this point in my life, one more problem would probably destroy me.

___ Total for Stage Six

How to Score Yourself: Add the number of checks in each of the stages. Totals higher than five in any of the stages indicate tendencies toward the Elvis Syndrome. Totals of four or more in consecutive stages indicate intervention at the foundation levels discussed in chapters nine and ten may be necessary. Totals of seven or more in any stage indicate areas that need to be addressed immediately.

Chapter 4

THAT'S ALL RIGHT, MAMA
THE ROLE OF FAMILY AND FRIENDS

"Nothing is so good as it seems beforehand."
— *George Eliot,* Silas Marner

It had been months since I'd last heard from Curtis. He had called earlier in the week and asked whether I would see him on Sunday. I readily agreed and looked forward to the meeting. Like most HAPs, he's quite protective of his privacy. He will meet me only at my home office and only on Sundays. On the days of his appointment, our understanding is that nobody will be scheduled the hour before or after his visit. That way there is no chance of him running into someone. He can't go shopping, to the movies, or even to a grocery store without people recognizing him, seeking autographs or just wanting to talk. Laughing about it, Curtis once paraphrased columnist and author Lewis Grizzard: "It's a lot like being married to a nymphomaniac. The first few months it's a lot of fun, but after a while it becomes a real problem." Like many of those experiencing death by success, Curtis had found notoriety can create massive pain.

And notoriety had certainly been a precipitating factor leading up to this appointment. To protect Curtis's identity, I can't describe precisely what had occurred. In general terms, he had received an award that involved a great deal of public and professional recognition. The publicity had been enormous. Though I rarely watch TV or listen to the radio, even I was aware of this occasion. During our telephone conversation, I congratulated him on the achievement.

"Hey. I hear kudos are in order." I bragged. "Way to go! It's great, man! I'm proud of you."

"Yeah." Curtis cleared his throat. "That's part of the problem. Well, sort of the problem. It's brought some things up."

"Oh, I'm sorry." I backpedaled. "Okay. Well . . . I'll look forward to seeing you."

"Me too," he responded. "It's been too long . . . ."

I left the conversation with a sense of curious foreboding. My fear at first was that his new accomplishment had led to a drinking episode. I thought about it for a few moments and finally decided I'd just have to wait and see. Finally, as I awaited him on Sunday, I reviewed several predictable things that could have gone wrong. But I didn't come close to anticipating what had occurred.

Curtis leaned over, elbows on his knees, staring blankly at the floor. He sighed deeply, tilting his head as he fidgeted with his ever present sunglasses. He tapped his foot rhythmically while clearing his throat and finally began to speak. "How do you remember all this stuff?" He smiled. "Doesn't all this run together after a while?"

"No." I smiled back. "I guess it's the sort of thing you develop a skill for. I mean, I don't know how you keep from getting words to songs mixed up. And chords to different music. I'd feel like a fool out there singing on stage."

"Yeah," he nodded. "Well, let me tell you why I'm here. You mentioned on the phone you'd heard about the award. And of course you know about the situation with my mother. And by the way, she's okay. She's doing fine. But this has brought up an entirely different reaction for me. How much do you remember about my dad?"

"Oh, me." I leaned forward. "Let's see. I remember he was gone all the time. He left your mom when you were thirteen or fourteen. He was in radio and television work. You told me you hadn't spoken to him in years. I don't know—fifteen or twenty years. But the last time you talked about him he was still alive and it seems like you had a couple of brothers by his second marriage that you'd never met."

Curtis nodded. "Actually, it's his third marriage. And I still haven't talked to him. I really thought he would call or make contact with me when he heard about the award. He's back in the music business now so I know he's aware of what's happened. It seemed to me this would be a convenient way for him to get in touch. He's not going to live forever. But anyway, a lot of things started coming back and I feel like I've done something awful wrong. It's almost like I feel guilty or wrong in some way. Something's just missing. I would like for him to at least call and just acknowledge that he's heard about it. It would make me feel better. Is that weird or what?"

Curtis went on to talk about a variety of memories that had resurfaced over the past several weeks. All of the troubling memories had to do with his father. "I'm a mama's boy," he'd informed me months earlier. "I love my mama. She's a saint to put up with what she did. Daddy, on the other hand, he's got some big problems." Like Elvis, Curtis had placed his mother on a pedestal. During his childhood, she overcompensated for his father's absence. And after his father left, they became even closer.

"For some reason," Curtis continued, "it's all coming to a head. I just can't seem to get it out of my mind that something's going to happen. I'd rather deal with all this while he's alive, than regret it when he's dead. I just can't get away from this idea that I've got to do something. Just the other night my great aunt told me I was just like him. I look like him. I sound like him. We're in the same business—sort of. And I hate it, but our personalities are still alike. I still do some of the stupid shit I hated so bad in him. We fought some of the same battles. Had a lot of the same problems. Thank God I don't have a son to pass all this on to, huh?" He laughed nervously, shaking his head. "This is not going to be easy, is it?" He leaned toward me as I somberly shook my head back and forth.

"No," I replied slowly. "No, it's not going to be easy at all."

"There's always one moment when the door opens and lets the future in."
—Graham Greene, The Power and the Glory

It's not impossible to escape the effects of early childhood modeling, but it's close. Today's society is filled with examples.

Some of them are even becoming the basis for important changes in the legal system and possibly legislation. The wealthy Menendez brothers, as an example, justified the murders of their parents by claiming child abuse during the early years of their lives. A lady in Sonora, California, was cleared of murder charges claiming she was molested twenty years earlier. Michael Fay, the young American who was whipped with a cane in Singapore, also used childhood problems as a basis for his appeal to be freed from jail. Each of these examples is legal justification, not scientific explanation. But they illustrate how acceptable the impact of childhood trauma has become.

The significance of childhood modeling is phenomenal. The role model a child watches daily has a marked impact on personality development later in adulthood. This in no way justifies the irrational behavior of people like the Menendez brothers. Nobody forced them to kill their parents. Their parents did not *model* homicide. It's ludicrous to even consider it. However, if the courts are hearing it at all, the point is made. Childhood influence does matter. And so does the power of the role model. Many scientific studies illustrate the point well, as does folk wisdom: "Like father like son," "The apple doesn't fall far from the tree." The Bible talks about the sins of the father being passed from one generation to another. Each of these is indirect commentary on the influence of modeling.

Scientists also seem to agree. There are various factors, as an example, contributing to teenage suicide. Drug use, peer pressure, and family problems all play a role in this tragedy. But of all the various factors, only one has a high degree of predictive validity. That one is *depression in the mother* of the child. Similar results were found in predicting children who had had problems with drug addiction. Once again, there are various contributing factors, but the most reliable one was found to be tranquilizer use in the mother of the child. And the same result is true of self-esteem in children. High self-esteem in the mother is more significant than any other single factor. The reason mothers play such a powerful role is that they are the primary caretakers of children. When dad is the primary caretaker, his influence is more powerful. If the role models are positive or constructive, so are the results. When they are negative, the results will likely be negative as well.

Research banks are filled with studies to back this up. It is true that people abused as children are more likely to become child abusers. Similarly, people raised rationally by their parents are far more likely to raise their children rationally. Men who grow up watching their fathers beat up their mothers are more likely to become wife beaters themselves. And people who grew up watching parents become involved in self-destructive behavior are certainly more likely to become self-destructive.

Curtis grew up watching his father abuse alcohol, beat his wife, and then leave the entire family. Eventually Curtis had some of the same problems. He even entered a career field similar to his father's. Elvis grew up closely attached to his mother, Gladys. In her book, *Elvis and Me*, Priscilla Presley implied Gladys had a fairly serious drinking problem. It appears through various reports she was chronically depressed after the death of Elvis's twin and never recovered. Regardless, she died young and the official diagnosis was heart failure after a long bout with hepatitis.

It is *possible* that Elvis grew up with a chronically depressed mother and psychologically unavailable father. There is evidence that Gladys developed a lifelong drinking problem after the twin's death, with hepatitis as a possible side effect. It is well-known that Gladys was Elvis's primary caretaker and his likely role model. Priscilla described Gladys as the "love of Elvis's life." They were very close. The similarities are frightening.

She died August 14, 1958. He died August 16, 1977.

She reportedly never got over Jesse's death. He apparently never got over her death.

She was depressed. He was depressed.

She had one child. He had one child.

She apparently had problems with alcohol. He apparently had problems with drugs.

Her official cause of death was heart failure. His official cause of death was cardiac arrhythmia.

She died at age forty-two. He was forty-two also.

The power of modeling is phenomenal.

"If you cannot get rid of the family skeleton,
you may as well make it dance."
—*George Bernard Shaw*

I'm not as filled with mother-love as Elvis. But as part of my own southern male heritage, I do have a great relationship with my own "Mama." In fact, she has been my best friend since I returned from Vietnam in 1971. I visited her and the rest of my extended family the weekend before my birthday in 1985. This particular trip I decided for some unknown reason to take Mark, my nephew, to see my father's burial site. My father died when I was only ten. Mark was born twelve years later. He had never seen the graveyard and was both curious and a bit intimidated by the tombstones.

"Why is he buried way out here?" Mark asked. My father's buried in a very rural area.

"It's where his family is," I explained. "I guess that's what he wanted. I really don't know."

"This is really strange." Mark said as he surveyed the grave-yard. He was only thirteen at the time. "What are we going to do?"

"I just wanted you to see his tombstone." I put my arm around him and patted his shoulder. "He was your grandfather. Even though you never got to know him, he's still a part of your life." I began looking at the different tombstones. It had been several years since I had been there. But I found my father's grave quickly.

"What was he like?" Mark asked. "What kind of person was he?" I began to answer, but I was interrupted by Mark. "Wow! He didn't live very long. Look at that. He was young. How old was he when he died?" Mark was pointing out the dates on the panel.

"Yeah." I frowned. "He was real young. I think he was only thirty-six when he died." I leaned over while doing the math. "Oh no." I groaned.

"What's wrong?" Mark backed up like he'd seen a ghost. "What's the matter?"

"He was only thirty-five when he died." I mumbled.

"So?" Mark shrugged. "What's the big deal, thirty-five or thirty-six, either way he was pretty young."

I turned, looking at Mark, and after a few seconds responded. "I turn thirty-five in three days." I shook my head. "I thought I was going to have a whole year to prepare."

Since beginning graduate school, I had anticipated this year. I couldn't remember then and still don't recall today when or where my concern originated. But I certainly believe in the power of modeling. And I didn't want to die at the same age as my father. I had been a part of many discussions concerning Elvis's death at the same age as Gladys. However, I'd planned on getting prepared for it in more detail. I had thought my father was thirty-six when he died, not thirty-five. Some have said if I had not "coincidentally" and unexpectedly taken time to visit the graveyard, I would have died that year. Bringing it to awareness led me to avoid any subconscious self destructive drive that I may have experienced. But with awareness comes responsibility. So within three days I contacted a variety of friends, all of whom were therapists, in southern California and purchased a ticket to Los Angeles. Two days of intense psychotherapy ensued. A tremendous number of memories, emotions, and insights arose during those marathon sessions.

The last several hours I was figuratively and literally in the middle of the most unusual therapy session of my life. Eight of my friends arranged their chairs in a circle and directed me to get in the middle. I was told to shut my eyes and relax. One of my former professors then took me through a standard relaxation technique very similar to hypnotic induction. When I reached a deeply relaxed level, all eight people began talking softly at the same time. Rather than becoming confused, I just relaxed even further. I was unable to consciously concentrate on any one thing being said, but could interpret a sentence here or a word there. After what seemed like fifteen or twenty minutes, I was asked to open my eyes. My former professor asked me how long the session had lasted. I suggested it lasted less than thirty minutes but told him I really wasn't sure. He smiled, paused a moment, and explained it had taken three and a half hours!

On April 12, 1986, I was in Chicago as guest on a local late-night radio talk show. It had been a few days less than a year since the weekend in Los Angeles. The talk show concluded at ll:00 p.m. and I walked back to my nearby hotel. "Tomorrow I'll be thirty-six," I thought to myself. I think I'm going to make it. I began reviewing all that had occurred that year. Frankly it had been a struggle. At various times I had thought I wasn't going to make it at all. I looked at my watch. It was 11:15 in Chicago, after midnight eastern time. I began to debate whether I should celebrate on April 13 in the eastern time zone, or Chicago time. Then I recalled my father had died in California—the pacific time zone! I finally decided to stay up until 2:01 a.m. central time and then had my own private party, including calling Bud and LA back in Chattanooga. Since my father had died in California and it was past midnight there, I felt safe.

They both, ironically, were awake awaiting my anticipated call. They had also been holding their breath. The power of modeling is phenomenal. In Chapter Two, I mentioned some people don't have permission to achieve at a higher level than their parents. Unfortunately, some people also don't have permission to live longer than their parents. The last therapy session I described was designed to give me that permission. My friends knew me well enough to realize my defense mechanisms were extremely powerful. By not being able to focus on any one voice, I was defenseless. For three-and-a-half hours my subconscious was bombarded with messages granting the permission I needed. I still don't recall much about what was said. At the same time, I don't have any childhood memories of anyone saying, "It's not okay for you to live longer than your father." Nor did anyone tell Curtis, "You can't achieve a higher level than your father." Certainly nobody told Elvis he needed to die at the same age as his mother. But somebody did need to warn him there was risk involved. Elvis and those around him were unaware of the significance of modeling. Don't you make the same mistake.

"As the twig is bent the tree inclines."
—Virgil (70-19 BC.)

There are other major influences occurring in early childhood contributing to the Elvis Syndrome. Modeling is the most significant, but there are others of vast importance. This is especially significant when the role model is absent or so erratic the child rejects it completely. Researchers have found, as an example, many people who have social and emotional problems as adults were raised in homes where logic did not apply. Regardless of what they did, these people were either consistently abused, or consistently overindulged. There has been tremendous focus in the past twenty years on abusive parenting, but very little on the opposite extreme. Yet as far back as 1966 and again in 1975, major research studies found both arbitrary acceptance and arbitrary rejection contributed to major personality flaws in adulthood. These flaws are the precise ones leading to death by success.

Albert De Salvo, known as the Boston Strangler, was one example of consistent over-abuse in childhood. Ted Bundy, on the other hand, who killed by some estimates over twenty young women, was an example of consistent overindulgence. Apparently both extremes teach children there is no connection between behavior and consequences. As a result, they become desensitized to normal social consciousness. Elvis was quite indulged by his mother. The same finding has occurred with almost all victims we have investigated who suffer the Elvis Syndrome.

An additional contributing factor to the Elvis Syndrome can also begin during childhood. Higher stage HAPs are far more likely than others to have lost a parent to death, separation, or abandonment. With this loss is a simultaneous void of affection and what some experts call parental deprivation. William McCord's 1964 study found this often leads to selfish, cynical, and unfeeling behavior. Each of these is manifested in the early and later stages of the Elvis Syndrome.

The final parenting consideration contributing to the Elvis Syndrome is the combination of parent personalities. It has already been stated that overly indulgent, doting mothers appear to foster tendencies toward self-destructiveness. Combined with a hypermasculine but emotionally unavailable father, the mixture

becomes almost toxic. Over ninety percent of stage six HAPs
I've interviewed have originated from this particular combination. Generally as young adults, HAPs leave home early to
escape toxicity. Occasionally, it's to attend college. However, in
over half the cases I've investigated, they left early to marry.

> *"If you do marry, you'll regret it.*
> *If you do not marry, you will also regret it."*
> *—Soren Kierkegaard*

As Curtis discussed the early relationship with his father,
things became more clear. "When he reached out his hand to
touch me, I never knew whether he was going to hit or hug me.
He wasn't there enough so that I could really get to know him. I
couldn't predict what he was going to do next. Then about the
time I thought I had him figured out, he was gone. I started
spending more time with my first wife's family because I thought
they seemed more normal. I guess I married her because of her
parents. I don't know . . . ."

Most advanced-level HAPs learn early in life to distrust emotions and fear closeness. The learning comes indirectly from living in such emotional chaos. They simultaneously long for closeness yet run from it due to enormous childhood fears. Like
Curtis, many search for stability in early marriages but seldom
succeed. Usually these relationships are misled attempts to
escape chaos and they commonly fail. Most HAPs will have a
long series of usually monogamous relationships. Some will
result in marriage. Others won't. But usually there is only one
relationship at a time. An advanced- level HAP virtually never
experiences only one marriage. It is equally rare for a HAP to be
carrying on more than one intense relationship at a time. Usually
they're too self-absorbed to expend that much energy on other
people.

This is not to say they don't have affairs. They usually do. But
they have them one at a time. Many HAPs remain in empty marriages for business or financial reasons. But those relationships
usually are empty, not intense. The HAP redirects his or her
intensity to the affair. HAPs who do remain married to the same

spouse will often have a series of long-term affairs, lasting the entire course of the marriage. These are usually sexually centered. Sex, either inside or outside the marriage, is used frequently by advanced-level HAPs as a drug. It's a way to hide from the pain or divert attention from problems. HAPs normally do not make love. They copulate or engage in a purely physical act that at its best is stress relieving. Regardless of the compulsive characteristics assigned to the sexual relationship, it can't be mistaken as an act of love. In advanced stages of the Elvis Syndrome, the ability to love is missing. It's probably been gone for years.

Just as a drug addict progresses from nicotine to marijuana to cocaine, the advanced stage HAP evolves from one sexually based relationship to another. Still looking for the same love and stability he did as a teen, the HAP has no idea how to find it. And with each successive relationship, he drifts further and further from truth. He remains in one relationship until the partner really gets to know him and then exits. He grows to fear people who know him since they also know his weaknesses, his mistakes, and his vulnerabilities.

> *"So we beat on, boats against the current,*
> *borne back ceaselessly into the past."*
> —*F. Scott Fitzgerald,* The Great Gatsby

It's not just parenting and marital relationships that appear emotionally cloudy for the HAP. Most of their relationships are dysfunctional. Since they rarely had a healthy primary attachment with anyone as children, they have difficulty trusting attachments now. Advanced-level HAPs *make* commitments regularly. They just can't *keep* them, and they direct the blame everywhere but toward themselves. In Chapter Three their tendency towards paranoia was discussed. At this point interpersonal paranoia becomes one of the primary personality features. As a result, he carries a high level of resentment, bitterness, and usually rage about the past. His immense level of unfinished hostility is ultimately projected to those around him. In time, the only people willing to remain around the HAP are those who are part of the entourage. Employees, roadies, and groupies become family. The only social commitment honored is one where the HAP maintains control through employment. This network of people serve and protect the HAP, but usually in a way that eventually leads to figurative and literal death by success. They become enablers. They enable the progressive loss of contact with reality. By insulating and isolating the HAP, they foster his delusional thinking. By covering up the HAP's irresponsibility, they indirectly encourage his or her drug and alcohol abuse. By trying to protect him or her from less-than-flattering feedback, they unintentionally contribute to the growing, cancerous arrogance. Often when confronted by staff, the HAP simply fires them. The consequences over time are delayed but escalate to the point that many simply can't face them. They run away, escape, or ultimately, like Elvis experience a premature death by success.

In the December 7, 1992 issue of *Newsweek*, an example is discussed from the life of Ernest Hemingway. The article described him as devastated after the demise of his third marriage. In response, Hemingway found a younger, more compliant wife. He drank even more, and killed himself at the age of sixty-one. Sometimes death seems a more desirable alternative than facing yourself in the eyes of someone who truly knows you. Someone who really knows you, however, could be a true friend and take a stance that might result in temporary pain or fear but long-term healing. A real friend would take this stance though he or she may risk losing the friendship for the benefit of your health.

One of my favorite parenting stories is about eagles, which bring new meaning to the empty-nest syndrome. When the mother eagle tires of her young crowding the nest, she figuratively and literally nudges him out. The young bird will drop from the nest, sometimes built hundreds of feet on the edge of a cliff. At some point the young bird either flaps his wings and flies away or is rescued by the hovering mother inches before crashing to the ground. A few eagles hit bottom before mom can reach them, but the number is quite low. The threat of "hitting bottom" most often results in the young eagle spreading his wings. He becomes suddenly independent and flies away on his own.

In Chapter One Curtis spoke of his own experience at hitting bottom when he woke up in Tucumcari, with no idea of how he had gotten there. For Curtis and others who dropped from such heights, the options become painfully clear. Straighten up and fly right, or crash and burn. Fly or die.

Luckily when Curtis returned from Tucumcari, his family and *healthy* friends welcomed him. They also insisted he get help. His wife orchestrated a meeting where Curtis was faced with himself. Like Luke Skywalker in the *Star Wars* saga, Curtis was forced to confront himself. Luke thought he was dueling Darth Vader. Curtis had thought everyone around him was the problem, not himself. Luke found he was his own worst enemy. So did Curtis.

The family member or friend who really wants to help needs to nudge the stage-six HAP toward reality. This sometimes means risking the fearful fall. But hitting bottom is not always bad. Curtis started getting well only after his crash. Elvis had family and friends around who loved him without question. They meant well and had only the best intentions. But they insulated him so intensely that he never had the opportunity to learn by suffering logical consequences. It's one of the great tragedies of his premature death, and likely one of the primary reasons for his fall.

Journal Session

1. Make a list of nicknames you received while growing up. Next to each one, briefly discuss how it made you feel and how it has influenced decisions in your life. Examples might include: "Bigfoot," "Newspaper," "Peacemaker," "Clumsy," etc. Even "positive" nicknames can affect you negatively. Being the "peacemaker" may have meant you were always expected to give in to keep up your "image."

2. List messages you received in the form of "You're just like__." List ways you actually *are* like the person named. Then list as many ways you are *not* like them. Discuss in writing the similarities that trouble you.

3. Examine why you left home. Discuss the possibility that you may have been running away from the situation there.

4. Many HAPs experience psychologically absent fathers. Discuss the availability of your own father and its impact on your childhood. Examine whether your mother may have tried to overcompensate for his absence. Discuss in writing your relationship with your parents over the years and examine whether your current relationship with them could benefit from some type of closure.

CHAPTER FOUR CHECKLIST

Directions: Check each one that applies.

____1. My father was absent during much of my growing years due to death, divorce, separation, or long hours on the job.

____2. I feel that my mother tried to make up for the loss of my father by being overprotective.

____3. I couldn't predict how my mother or father were going to react in a given situation. Sometimes they might punish me. At other times nothing would happen.

____4. I left home at an early age.

____5. A main reason I left home was to escape a "crazy home life."

____6. I have been or am currently involved in an extra-marital affair.

____7. I have been in a relationship, or am currently in a relationship that I maintain primarily for business or financial reasons.

____8. I have been divorced more than once.

____9. I am estranged from most of my family.

____10. I've been told by more than one family member that I am "just like my father, my grandfather, my mother, my grandmother," etc.

___TOTAL

How to Score Yourself: Add the number of checks. The higher the number of checks the higher the risk for the Elvis Syndrome. Totals above five indicate risk. You may wish to discuss these issues with another adult. Totals of seven or more are troubled scores and should probably be addressed by a clergyperson or mental health professional.

Chapter 5

IT'S NOW OR NEVER
THE ROLE OF THE
OBSESSIVE-COMPULSIVE PERSONALITY

"Let us not underestimate the privileges of the mediocre. As one climbs higher, life becomes even harder; the coldness increases; responsibility increases."
—*Friederick Nietzche*, The Antichrist

Death by success takes on many forms. You don't have to be an actor, professional athlete, or high-level sales representative to experience the Elvis Syndrome. You actually don't need a career at all. You simply have to achieve. Achievement, as noted before, could be getting promoted from minimum wage to twenty-five cents per hour above minimum. It could be making the finals in your local racquetball tournament. Or it could be accomplishing a personal goal you had worked on and planned for some time.

MDWIFE had struggled with obesity for most of her adult life. In elementary school and junior high she had excelled in dance. Through the eighth grade her life revolved around ballet, tap, and jazz. She had always been one of the most fit and lean people in her class. She had even started student teaching for her dance instructor in the eighth grade when her father was unexpectedly transferred. They moved from Tampa to Charlotte, so continuing to train with the previous instructor was impossible. She had difficulty fitting in with the new instructor and after several weeks gave up in exasperation.

She became depressed and began eating more than she had before. In the ninth grade, at five and a half feet tall, she went from one hundred ten to one hundred fifty pounds. By the time she graduated from high school, she had soared to one hundred eighty pounds. During her second pregnancy she peaked at two hundred thirty-eight pounds at the same height. Postpartum depression made things worse and this, combined with the other factors mentioned earlier, led to her divorce from MD.

During the divorce, she entered psychotherapy, began an aerobics class, and started going to Weight Watchers—all within a two-week period. She decided to start her life over again and within a year had lost sixty pounds. Six months later she weighed one hundred thirty pounds and had lost almost ninety pounds since beginning her new life. She had the job she wanted, the body she wanted, and was doing well as a single parent. She had achieved her goals and felt great.

She is very attractive and predictably received much attention from men. Most of it was superficial, harmless flirting. She had no trouble handling that sort of attention and actually enjoyed it. But one gentleman became more than a flirt. It was obvious he was interested and persistent. Though admittedly frightened, she allowed herself to grow emotionally closer, and eventually they became sexually involved. The relationship progressed and they began discussing marriage.

MDWIFE explained the weight change happened suddenly. The way she describes it, she went to bed one night weighing one hundred thirty and got up the next morning weighing one hundred fifty. It certainly took longer. But within three months she had gained twenty more pounds. Her weight gain had become an issue in their relationship. Additionally, she had begun ignoring her hair and personal grooming. After an intense discussion with her new live-in fiancé, she returned to psychotherapy.

I had lost contact with her over the years. After some discussion, however, it was fairly obvious what was happening. MDWIFE is a fairly compulsive, perfectionistic, and controlling person. If she is going to do something, she's going to do it well. When she danced as a child, she *really* danced. After moving from Tampa and beginning her weight gain, she *really* gained weight. When she decided to lose the extra weight, she really lost it, including an additional two hundred twenty pounds of worthless MD. She became an exercise fanatic and before meeting her fiancé was working out three hours per day. She was a person who thought if something's worth doing, then do it all the way. Do it right, do it perfectly, or don't do it at all. That included relationships. And that was the origin of her near death by success.

MDWIFE's previous marriage had been disastrous. She had told me dozens of times she would never remarry. She had no intention of growing close to any man, much less getting engaged. Regardless of what she wanted, no relationship could be perfect. And even though her fiancé was loving and cooperative, she could not control him. Like most perfectionists, she decided subconsciously if it couldn't be perfect she simply would not have a relationship at all. It wasn't simply a thought. It was a decision made below her level of awareness. She wanted a decent marriage but her fear of failure was stronger than her desire for closeness. As a way of avoiding conflict, MDWIFE made an additional subconscious decision. She would let her fiancé end the relationship based on her weight gain. She would run him off but let him initiate the breakup. Then she could once again be a victimized woman—fat, lonely, and depressed. It was the Elvis Syndrome in classic form. But it didn't work. She was able to turn herself around and avoid further self-sabotage.

"Nothing is sufficient for the person who finds sufficiency too little."
—*Epicurus in* The Philosophy of Epicurus *by G. K. Stroddach*

I have worked with literally hundreds of HAPs as a consultant over the years. By organizing and cataloging my observations, I found there were differences in the habits and personalities of people who achieve on a large scale. This is not necessarily true for those who make smaller achievements. It is definitely true for those who achieve major accomplishments, suffer tremendous setbacks, and then achieve once again. Some of those who experience such patterns are simple business failures. Others experience the Elvis Syndrome on multiple occasions. McDonald's founder Ray Kroc and Walt Disney went through several corporate bankruptcies. Yet they both kept on achieving and ultimately were extremely successful in spite of their setbacks.

Andy Warhol commented, "Everyone experiences fifteen minutes of fame." The fascinating group, however, are those who experience even longer moments of fame without self-destructing or going through the same cycles MDWIFE did. In my observations of successful HAPs, several attitudes become clear. The basic requirement is obviously talent. Each HAP I've interviewed has extraordinary skill and talent within his or her area of expertise. In most cases this talent surfaced quite early. Some seemed to be child prodigies. Their skill, even in childhood, can appear almost surreal. The HAP makes work appear easy, regardless of its complexity. You will often hear comments describing the HAP as "naturals." People claim they have God-given talent. Others describe them as "gifted." HAPs appear to be all of those things. Yet in many ways such descriptions are insults. Their compliments ignore the other necessary qualities to become a HAP. Talent alone is nothing more than potential. Discipline to develop the talent, however, can make it something more than potential.

For talent to turn into achievement, discipline must be applied. It takes a substantial degree of work to polish talent and discipline makes it possible. Discipline is the ingredient that results in the HAP being task-oriented long enough to apply the remaining characteristics. In all the HAPs I've interviewed, discipline was obvious. The next quality most successful HAPs have is work ethic. What we most often misinterpret as natural ability is actually the result of literally thousands of hours of work. Though the HAP makes it look easy, people probably haven't looked at the amount of time they've spent in practice. As observers we see a fifteen-year-old gold-medalist swimmer and think "how sweet" or "how cute." But what we overlook is the same athlete has probably practiced a minimum of three to six hours a day for nearly twelve years. This athlete has actually swam somewhere between ten thousand and twenty thousand hours for the championship competition. That's the equivalent of ten years of forty-hour work weeks. This has been her full-time job for ten years! That's not natural. That's work and persistence. The work is almost always overlooked.

*"If people knew how hard I have to work to gain my mastery,
it wouldn't seem wonderful at all."*
—*Michaelangelo, Italian painter and sculptor*

Many rock music fans assume The Grateful Dead's Jerry Garcia is a born performer. Actually, Garcia's talent is a result of the same work and persistence the gold-medalist swimmer demonstrated. Garcia explains that as a child he was not good at music at all. He was forced to take piano lessons for eight years. Discipline came from his mother and grandmother. On Saturday nights they used to sit with Jerry and listen to the Grand Ole Opry. Garcia estimates he heard bluegrass maestro Bill Monroe hundreds of times during his early youth. Beginning in about 1960 the discipline became internalized. It was learning banjo that turned him around.

At age fifteen, he began playing the guitar after receiving one as a birthday present. At that point he started practicing without any encouragement from anyone. Today he is a member of one of the most durable rock groups ever. With Garcia and all HAPs, it's work and persistence that pays off, not natural talent.

Successful HAPs also have a passion for what they do. When a HAP discusses his work, his face changes. His eyes light up as he leans forward. The typically quiet HAP becomes a chatterbox. He may work tirelessly at his task without any sign of fatigue. As a husband or father he may be a bore. But at his chosen task, the HAP grows intensely passionate. Instead of expending energy, the HAP appears to get energized by working harder and longer hours. They enjoy working so much, most would do it for free. Elvis, in fact, sang for his supper many years before getting paid. Even after the release of *That's All Right, Mama*, he sang for free on several occasions.

Many HAPs seem eccentric to others and at times appear to be involved in almost superstitious rituals. A September 20, 1994, article in *USA Today* described San Francisco 49ers' Jerry Rice's behavior prior to football games. It takes him three hours just to put on his uniform, a normal twenty minute process. He polishes his helmet, wears only new socks and new shoes, and is meticulous in his preparation. He has an elaborate series of rituals surrounding the fitting of his socks, pants, wristbands, and jersey. When he gets everything just right, he tapes it into place. During this process, he's building an intensity level, which helps him focus on the game. It must work. He is an incredibly focused athlete. Curtis reported similar rituals prior to his concert dates. These rituals began three hours prior to his stage appearance. He prays three times, for exactly three minutes. Each prayer must begin at the top of the hour. He changes clothes three times before going on stage, and insists the number of clothing articles he's wearing is divisible by three. These eccentricities apply to him only on concert dates. Like Jerry Rice, Curtis uses these rituals to get ready for performances.

There are many qualities contributing to the evolution of a HAP. Most have been discussed thus far. For a high-performing individual to become a HAP, however, a final quality must be mastered. The HAP must either form a partnership to *expand his influence* or develop marketing-related skills on his own. Bo Jackson and Michael Jordan both had Nike money and the best advertising agencies in the world to make them household names. Elvis had Colonel Tom Parker. You can speculate infinitely what one would have been without the other. As a team, they made a phenomenal impact. There is literally no one to compare the Colonel to today, just as there is no relationship theirs can be compared to. The Colonel was a very complex man. He was part psychologist, part business partner, and part father to Elvis. He promoted Elvis like no one has been promoted before or since. He used midgets, elephants, billboards, gossip, double-talk, manipulation, and even threats to further the King's career. As a result, both were enriched.

The Colonel expanded Elvis's influence. Marketing is not the key in all HAPs' careers. But expansion is. In some endeavors, marketing is not necessary at all. Perhaps capital is needed. Perhaps it is technical skill, sales background, or manufacturing knowledge. There is normally one missing ingredient in a HAP's development. As an example, any cook can make a batch of good cookies. But few people can expand their cookies to become "Famous Amos." Most people can shoot a basketball. But there is only one Michael Jordan. There have been a lot of singers, but there was only one Elvis. The difference between the superstar and others is the ability to expand their influence. For a HAP to become a superstar, influence such as the Colonel's is necessary. It's unlikely that any HAP could accomplish this alone.

The minds and habits of achievers are fascinating. If their behavior and attitudes could be put in a pill, you would probably be willing to take it. But you would need an antidote to the poison of The Elvis Syndrome. The final skill I've noted in HAPs who avoid the Elvis Syndrome is a fail-safe mechanism. It's a plan to prevent them from experiencing death by success. This is discussed further in a future chapter.

> *"To do all that one is able to do is to be a man;*
> *to do all that one would like to do is to be a god."*
> *—Napoleon I*

A women once spotted Pablo Picasso in a Paris restaurant. After building up her courage for twenty minutes, she finally approached his table. "Maestro," she gushed. "I adore your work. You're magnificent. Here—take my napkin and draw anything on it. Please." She thrust it at Picasso. He took the napkin, scribbled something out for a few minutes, and then gave it back. "That will be fifty thousand dollars," he told her.

"But, Maestro," she objected. "It only took you three minutes."

"No." He shook his head. "You don't understand. It took my entire life."

HAPs do make their art look easy. It's difficult for others to appreciate the length of time it took Picasso and others to develop their skill. It cannot be overemphasized how intensely they work. MDWIFE exercised three hours per day and limited her daily food intake to fifteen hundred calories. After she had maintained her weight loss for several months, people began telling her how lucky she was to have a high metabolism! Curtis won his first talent show at the age of four. His father was taking him to the Grand Ole Opry in Ryman Auditorium even before that. As a six-year-old he sat in on jam sessions with bluegrass bands. For show and tell in the second grade, he played four different songs in class on four different instruments. But while other kids practiced ball, he practiced music. Practice makes the high-achiever successful. And it takes tremendous time.

The characteristics of HAPs mentioned earlier were from observations I have made in my interviews. Other studies have discovered additional qualities in those who achieve at a high level. These qualities are taken from various sources and are synthesized in the next few pages. Some are similar to those already discussed. Others are different. All have referred to achievement in general and make no distinction between those who later experience death by success and those who don't.

One study found achievers have a strong sense of purpose. They are strongly convinced their life work is meaningful. There is an overwhelming and almost spiritual belief that life is important on a large scale, and each hour of each day is purposeful on a small scale. Because achievers experience such a strong sense of purpose, it's easier for them to develop a healthy degree of self-confidence. Not only do HAPs believe that their life is purposeful, but they're every bit up to the challenge. At times they appear to have a missionary zeal and indeed many suggest their lives are controlled by a higher power. Each of these qualities is synthesized by the HAP's unique ability to organize his or her life and manage time. They make lists, schedules, and goals. Their time is spent responding to plans and objectives rather than impulse. In my work with HAPs, this last quality appears to be the *defining* one among the three that separate those who experience death by success from those who don't.

Impulse may suggest various self-destructive behaviors. Responding to it is the same as responding to Freud's *id* mentioned in Chapter Three. When the drive of achievement creates pressure and anxiety, impulse will dictate seeking pleasure and pressure relief. It can be consuming too much alcohol, taking drugs, or withdrawing and insulating in a negative way. It can also be overeating, gambling compulsively, or smoking too much. The impulse wants to be gratified. Delaying gratification and being driven by organized goals and objectives is one of the traits that can prevent the Elvis Syndrome. In most cases, it's succumbing to the gratification of these impulses that opens the door to the journey of self-sabotage.

"Is there anything in life so disenchanting as attainment?"
—*Robert Louis Stevenson,* The New Arabian Nights

"You're only as good as your last three deals." The man I call Topanga Jack sat across from me beside his wife, Tanya. He was thirty-nine when the conversation took place but looked much older. He glanced over at his wife tensely then back toward me. "I've been through all this before. It really sucks. But it's the only way I know I can make a lot of money. In the late '70s I developed real estate in southern California. In one year I went from a mansion on Mulholland Drive to living in a fifteen-foot trailer in Topanga Canyon. It's that kind of business.

"Now we've run into problems with the golf resort. The greens are a mess. But it's weather. You know—there's nothing you can do to change it. Then the south Florida development went down with Hurricane Andrew. I'm trying to buy a hotel in Hilton Head, but I'm having problems putting that deal together because of what happened with Camille and Andrew. I don't have anything to do with the damn weather, but it seems to have some kind of karmic problem with me." Topanga Jack laughed nervously, twitching his head back and forth. He looked down at the floor, as he fought back tears for the second time since he began talking.

"Tanya is not criticizing you or putting you down." I spoke up to ease his tension level. "She's never complained or said anything negative. In fact, she has been very complimentary of you." I leaned toward Topanga Jack and rested my elbows on my knees. "She's not attacking you. I'm not attacking you. There's really nothing to defend. You're not being accused of anything. She just wants more of your time. And she's concerned about you smoking and drinking more. That's all it is. She just loves you." He looked first at Tanya, then back at me, turned his back to both of us and started crying softly.

Topanga Jack had been showing most of the symptoms listed in Chapter Two and was approaching stage six of the Elvis Syndrome. Tanya had been married to him for seven years and met Jack when he returned from California. His career had taken off again about the time they met and for the past several years it had boomed. Topanga Jack specializes in developing ocean front resort property and golf courses. He excelled at it and made an enormous amount of money for his investors and himself. He admits to being a workaholic who loves his business and he is definitely in control of almost everything. But he can't control the weather. Hurricane Camille had destroyed one of his resorts on Hilton Head. Hurricane Andrew devastated his golf course in south Florida. Other bad weather in the Florida panhandle had destroyed the greens on his golf resort. Investors became cautious and frightened of what might happen next. "You're only as good as your last three deals," he reminded me.

Like most HAPs, Topanga Jack is extremely obsessive-compulsive. He's somewhat rigid, over-conscientious, and very concerned with conformity and approval from others. "If my investors are happy and everybody likes the resorts, then I'm fine," he explained. "But if they're miserable, then so am I. If this streak of weather continues, I'll be a complete failure." Jack is extremely meticulous and hardworking. Like most obsessive-compulsives who choose the right profession, he's also quite successful. But he has strong inhibitions against expressing emotions and tremendous difficulty relaxing. So he drinks to medicate his tense emotions and smokes to help him relax. He'd not spoken to Tanya about the business problems until she pressed him in psychotherapy, though Camille had struck many years earlier.

The word *obsessive* refers to an idea or thought. *Compulsion* refers to an urge to action that can result in repetitive behavior patterns. Combining these two qualities creates a person who's often driven in an almost single-minded way to do something. Obsessive-compulsive energy is extremely powerful. Like the Energizer Bunny, they "keep going and going." Obsessive-compulsives probably built America and certainly built industry. Leaders in any organization are likely to have this kind of personality. If you think of a highly successful person, you probably will be seeing an obsessive-compulsive. They are generally hardworking and driven, and they tirelessly pursue the object of their obsession. They aren't Type A. They're Type A-plus!

Every corporate boardroom, courtroom, and surgical room in the world is likely to be occupied and mastered by obsessive-compulsives. They are capable of focusing enormous energy on their business, law practice, or medical career, and often become very successful and wealthy. At the same time every Salvation Army mission room, every alcohol and drug rehab room and counseling room at a psychiatric hospital is also filled with this personality type. There are highly functional and constructive aspects to the obsessive-compulsive personality. There can be extremely destructive ones as well.

The motto of an obsessive compulsive is "Nothing in Moderation." If anything is worth doing, it's worth doing in excess! When Topanga Jack changed coasts to start a real-estate development, he did well. When MDWIFE decided to lose weight, she exercised three hours per day and counted her calories rigorously. She ate *exactly* fifteen hundred calories. There were charts, food logs, graphs, and every imaginable entry in her weight-loss diary, And when they decide to drink or use drugs, gamble, or focus on sex, obsessive compulsive achieve the same success. Whatever the obsessive compulsive does, he or she will do well. This is a very important consideration, because to become a HAP, you must get obsessed with success. It's simply impossible to succeed at a high level and achieve superstar status without becoming overwhelmingly focused on your goal. This is true, whether it's in business, athletics, or entertainment. It's equally true when your goal is less grandiose, such as losing weight. You must become obsessed. At the same time, this is where the potential danger lies. It's similar to approaching "critical mass." While it's necessary to become obsessed to succeed at a very high level, it's the same obsessiveness leading to the Elvis Syndrome. It is a necessary ingredient to be a superstar. It is also a necessary ingredient for death by success.

"To achieve great things we must live   *as*
though we were never going to die."
—Marquis de Vauvenargues, Reflections and Maxims

The roller-coaster journey to success, described earlier by Topanga Jack, is not that uncommon. It's the unusual person who can absorb such change without giving up. When the door on the west coast was slammed in his face, Jack began knocking on the east-coast door. And like many HAPs, he knocked until someone opened it, even if ever so slightly. It's not that he might be tempted to give up easily. An obsessive-compulsive Type A would never do that. The problem is that they come to see the roller coaster as being common and expected. Sometimes if it is not there, they actually create it! I suggested to Jack that perhaps the swing wasn't inevitable, though it had happened before.

"Is there even the slightest possibility," I suggested, "things could be more level?"

"Oh no," he declared. "Something will definitely go wrong . Everything is a huge disaster or a huge success. It's never anything in between. Honest to God, one week I was living in a mansion. Three weeks later to the day, I was driving a '65 Ford station wagon and living in a fifteen-foot trailer in a buddy's backyard in Topanga Canyon. I took a shower by hanging a hose out the window and standing underneath it. Then I'd put on one of those thousand-dollar suits I'd saved from the good times and be out hustling again. That's just normal to me. Something bad is *always* going to happen."

Living with this belief is one of the adverse side effects found with most HAPs obsessed with success. It creates a great deal of anxiety and is probably somewhat responsible for the large number of stress-related disorders HAPs experience.

Jack also discussed a second side effect of becoming obsessed with success. The desire for others' approval is a major drawback. Many HAPs define their worth and importance by how intensely others need them. This is actually a twisted version of the desire for control. Jack suggested that if others are pleased with his work, then he's happy. If people invest their money in his projects, they need him. He's then in control and perceives himself as more worthwhile. However, his earlier comment describes the outcome: "You're only as good as your last three deals" (or your last interception or your last recording, etc.).

An additional adverse side effect is found with those who become obsessed with success and approach stages five or six. Those around the HAP and ultimately the HAP himself begin to assume mastery. A collective assumption is made that the same skill and ability that brought success in one area can be transferred to life at large. Since F. Scott Fitzgerald could write, for example, he should be capable of making decisions about his drinking. If Donald Trump could develop real estate, he should also be able to develop a great marriage. Since Mike Tyson could box, he should be able to manage his personal life. This process is very dangerous. Complacent trust in the HAP's ability to master life is a deadly assumption. Yet this assumed mastery is found by almost all HAPs and those who associate with them.

Occasionally the consequences of assumed mastery can take on complicated and paradoxically troubling twists. "Cow Pies," mentioned earlier, found this in his own divorce. The judge, well aware of Cow Pies' popularity, was shocked when looking at his financial statement. The judge simply refused to believe his tax returns could be such a mess. "Your honor," the anchorman told him, "I'm a news anchor, not an accountant. The problem is my accountant is also the plaintiff. The woman who did my taxes is sitting over there now divorcing me. She's the person I'd normally ask these questions of. Now I can't!" This was true. Cow Pies had married his accountant and now she was divorcing him. I know as a fact he is illiterate when it comes to finances. But the judge was not convinced. He, like others, assumed if someone can master TV news he can also master a tax form. It was a mistake on the judge's part. But it cost Cow Pies approximately double what he should have been required to pay in child support. The mistake is not about a tax form however. It's about assumed mastery. If you can master television, I assume you can master a tax form.

A surprising finding leading to the final side effect is that most HAPs tend to be introverted rather than extroverted. On the surface, especially with highly successful salespeople or performers, they appear quite outgoing. But usually the opposite is true. They wear the outgoing personality, like a suit of clothing. Deep inside they're very introverted. Introversion is not a problem. It is simply an orientation. But being introverted while living an extroverted life is a big problem. It leads to insecurity and ultimately an energy drain. Extroverts get energized being around others. Introverts expend energy being around others. There's a big difference. Introverts are quite sensitive and creative. But this also leads to a great deal of self-questioning. Removed from the individual time alone to energize herself, the introverted HAP can begin obsessing with self-analysis and grow even more insecure.

By becoming addicted to success, the HAP develops an even more destructive drive. It is virtually impossible to succeed at this level without also becoming obsessed with competing against others. This necessarily leads to an almost primal focus on dominating and winning. Isolation and suspicion will naturally result from such an attitude. Life grows to be viewed as a constant battle, and the HAP is viewed as a persistent threat. Eventually, a distorted, sick view of life begins to develop. For others to fail is for the HAP to win. Everyone, as a result , becomes a potential enemy, and in time nobody can be trusted. It becomes an endless and painful cycle ultimately leading to grossly pathological perfectionist tendencies. They develop impossible standards and begin to believe that not reaching them means failure. This kind of dichotomous thinking is always self defeating. Since he can't reach perfection, often the HAP will simply discontinue the activity. This results in many HAPs resigning from positions soon after getting promoted. Others walk off stage because the sound system doesn't work perfectly. Many actually commit suicide because of their fear, as F. Scott Fitzgerald said, "that you'll never be as good again."

> *"It had long since come to my attention that people of all accomplishment*
> *rarely sit back and let things happen to them.*
> *They went out and happened to things."*
> —Eleanor Smith

The term *addiction* comes from the Latin root *addictus* which means slave. An obsession is normally not an addiction in the technical sense. You become addicted when you develop a bio-chemical dependency on a drug. Theoretically you can't get addicted to work, but you can become a workaholic. Gambling isn't technically addictive, but I've seen dozens of people in psychotherapy who would swear they're addicted to it. You can't get addicted to shopping, but I know there are people out there who describe themselves as shopaholics.

Many years ago, while working in a psychiatric hospital, I had an experience that changed how I defined *addiction*. I was speaking with Ron, a lab technician, preparing to draw blood from a new patient. I didn't know it at the time, but Susan, the patient, had been addicted to heroin for several years.

I glanced at her while Ron prepared the syringe. Her eyes were fixed, trance-like, on Ron's hands. I watched closely as her breathing quickened. She soon began gasping audibly. After searching several seconds for a vein, Ron finally inserted the syringe. As the needle slowly penetrated her skin, Susan screamed aloud. Her skin flushed as sweat formed on her forehead. I thought she was about to faint and started to get out of my chair.

"Oh, she's okay, John," Ron drawled casually. "This is fun for her. Junkies love needles. She's getting off on it."

Later, after several weeks of treatment, Susan explained that although Ron's assessment was crude, it was nonetheless accurate. She had in fact experienced an orgasm the moment Ron inserted the syringe. On many occasions, unable to get heroin, she would insert an empty syringe under her skin and pump it. On some occasions, she explained, this resulted in a high, and on others a sexual response. While it's impossible to become technically addicted or romantically attached to a needle, Susan and thousands of others have done so.

Can we become obsessed with success? I say yes. Can we become addicted to success? Theoretically, no. In reality, however, I would say yes on this as well. Curtis described such an example in Chapter One. At the same time I think you can become addicted to food, gambling, sex, or almost any other activity. It's a devastating process.

"No great thing is created suddenly."
—Epictetus

MDWIFE was ultimately able to deal with her fear of closeness. She also was able to keep her weight under control. Yet this is something she will probably continue to struggle with for the rest of her life. The Elvis Syndrome is not contracted by a virus or by being bitten by a female anopheles mosquito. You don't get it by someone sneezing on you or by not washing your hands. The Elvis Syndrome is a result of intense and long-term learning.

Topanga Jack has also been able to control his tendencies toward the Elvis Syndrome. He and Tanya are still married, yet his self-destructive habits sometimes surface again. When he feels tense, he distances, insulates, and drinks more. When MDWIFE becomes fearful, she overeats and "forgets" to take showers. These are anxiety-reducing techniques that become very self-destructive.

You probably have similar self-destructive habits. They may be similar or different from those discussed in this chapter. The material is only as useful as you make it. Apply this material and you can manage your behavior and ultimately control your life. It's easy to focus on others. The test, however, is the ability to focus on yourself and avoid death by success in your life. MDWIFE works on this every day. Topanga Jack and Cow Pies do the same. You need to do it as well.

JOURNAL SESSION

1. Describe a time in your life when you were involved in repetitive or redundant types of behavior. As an example, MDWIFE had a problem with a redundant weight gain. Cow Pies had a history of losing jobs after promotions. Describe a similar pattern that you find recurring your life. Try to isolate one or two reasons that might be leading you to perpetuate your behavior.

2. Describe what you consider to be present or lacking in your life regarding discipline. Discipline was defined in this chapter as the ability to remain task-oriented long enough to apply your talent and ambition toward achieving your goals. Define whether enough discipline is present in your life. If not, describe why you believe it's important to develop more discipline.

3. It's common to observe skilled athletes or musicians and think "how lucky they are." As discussed in this chapter, most people forget about the work that has gone into making these people lucky. Describe something at which you may be skilled that others perceive as being lucky or gifted. Discuss the amount of work required to make you an artist at what you do.

4. Assumed mastery is dangerous. Recall when you were granted assumed mastery by others. Some high-achieving teenagers have this experience when their parents assume that because they have a perfect grade-point average they will automatically know when to end a date. Write about another occasion when you assumed someone else had mastery. Discuss the consequences of each incident.

CHECKLIST

Directions: The four areas below represent foundations that are important to HAP development. They are also helpful in preventing the Elvis Syndrome. Rate each question from zero (does not apply to me at all) to five (applies to me much of the time).

TALENT

___1. Have you been told by friends and associates that you have a "gift"?

___2. Do you excel in an area or areas that others find difficult to master?

___3. Are there other areas at which you are totally inept?

___4. Do you believe others could do what you do if only they would apply themselves and work as hard as you have?

___5. Do you use your gift often?

DISCIPLINE

___1. Do you dedicate a specific time regularly to developing your talent?

___2. Are you able to ignore the telephone or other "urgent" requests during this time?

___3. Do you have specific short-range goals for improvement?

___4. Do you have specific long-range goals for improvement?

___5. Have you been able to accomplish these goals?

PASSION

___1. I have chosen to use my gift as my major income-producing avenue, or am working toward that goal.

___2. Though I get tired like everyone else, I am energized when I use my talent.

___3. I have rituals associated with my performance. I write, (paint, compose, dance, etc.) in a special place, with special clothes, using a special pen, etc.

___4. I gain focus and intensity by using rituals.

___5. I am either using my talent without getting paid or would do so if I couldn't make a living at it.

SENSE OF PURPOSE

___1. I feel deeply that I have a responsibility to use my talent to help humankind.

___2. I know I am capable of doing good both for humankind generally and for family and friends through the use of my abilities.

___3. I know my time is important and endeavor to focus on "my purpose." I do not allow unimportant crises to interfere with the proper use of my time and talent.

___4. Others have accused me of being out-of-touch with reality for being so focused on the big picture.

___5. I feel I have a unique purpose to fulfill.

___ Total

How to Score Yourself: Total your score. The higher the score on this questionnaire, the healthier you probably are. Scores of less than fifty suggest weak foundations. Use the writing session to help you determine where you need work.

Chapter 6

CLIMB ABOARD THE MYSTERY TRAIN
THE INFLUENCE OF ALCOHOL AND DRUGS

"What is dangerous about the tranquilizers is that whatever peace of mind they bring is a packaged peace of mind. Where you buy a pill and buy peace with it, you get conditioned to cheap solutions instead of deep ones."
—*Max Lerner, "The Assault on the Mind"*
From The Unfinished Country *(1959)*

"I t's my brother. I'm really concerned about him and I'm not sure what to do." It seemed like I'd heard it all before. I was the guest on a radio talk show in St. Louis. The studio was larger than what I'm used to. There were eight chairs, eight microphones, and eight headsets at a large, round table in the middle of the studio. There I was alone. The announcer was in another room, separated by a double-glass window. We were able to make eye contact and give each other hand signals.

"Tell me about your brother," I prompted the caller. "What's going on that bothers you?"

"Well," she began, "It's been going on for years. He drinks. Not all the time though. But he'll pull a drunk once or twice a year. And he'll go on for a week or two at a time. I just don't know how to help him."

"Okay," I responded. "You're saying your brother goes on binges one or two times a year. Tell me, Caller, what has your family tried so far that has or has not helped? And, by the way, tell me more about your family. How old is your brother? Do you all live together? Fill me in on some of the background." I enjoy radio talk shows. I specifically enjoy those late at night. People seem more real. Talk is intimate. Insomniacs seem to be more honest about themselves in the middle of the night.

"No. He lives with his own family," she answered. "He'll be forty-one in May. I'm three years older than him. He's got two children by this marriage and one by his first. He's a good person, and he works real hard. There's no problem there. He can always find work. Of course, he loses his job when he goes on those drunks. Really, his only problem is the drinking."

"Okay," I shook my head. "Now, what have you tried that's helped or not helped? And what about his wife? How is she involved?"

"Oh, she's great!" the caller assured me. "She's real good to him. They don't have that many problems. She has a time with him when he's drinking. But that's about it. We've all talked to him about getting help, but he won't. He's gone to AA a couple of times, but he hates cigarette smoke, so he quit. My mom and dad talk to him a lot. But you can't talk to him at all when he's drunk. So really, nothing has helped at this point."

"Okay," I began. "First of all, I want you to know this is a fairly common story. He's not in this alone, for sure." There are many drinking and drug-use patterns. This sounded like a classic binge-drinking cycle. One of the things I've discovered over the years is there always seems to be a precipitating event leading to the binge. The binge appears to be a reaction to something stressful. The radio-show host asked the caller to hang on through the commercial break. She cooperated and then continued her call.

"Yeah, that's true for him," she agreed. "It always happens when it looks like things are going to be just great. Things are going to be at their brightest. Then boom! He's gone for three days and when he comes back home, he's drunk as hell and stays out of work for the rest of the week. Then he gets fired. This last time he'd just got promoted to used-car sales manager. Just got promoted! The day he was supposed to go in and start his new job, he's gone."

As I spoke to the caller, the picture became more clear. Her brother was actually experiencing a long-term case of the Elvis Syndrome. He was able to handle mediocrity just fine. But when the opportunity for relative success was presented, he would experience a near death by success. The same pattern had occurred two other times. He was indeed a very hard worker. He would start out at the bottom and, through sheer hard work and wit, quickly climb the ladder of success. About the time he was ready to get a major promotion, he would go on a binge, lose the promotion and the job. Then he would start over again somewhere else.

Once again he would start at the bottom and repeat the cycle. He had taken a job as a soft-drink route driver and worked hard for two years. During this period, he had not missed a day's work. He was rewarded by being promoted to district supervisor. To celebrate, she explained, he went on a binge and lost his job. He started over delivering newspapers. In less than a year, he was promoted to district distribution manager. Again, he went on a binge with the same result. The car sales job followed, and the pattern continued. The cycle seemed to repeat itself over and over again. It happened with her brother. It also happens with someone else's father, and another person's wife. It happens with alcohol. But it also occurs with cocaine and prescription drugs. However, in my opinion, it has very little to do with drugs at all. It's about the Elvis Syndrome.

In most cases, problems like this are treated as alcohol or drug addiction. The caller kept explaining, "The only problem is he drinks. If he would just quit drinking, everything would be fine." It really does seem like a drinking problem. And on the surface it appears that alcohol is the culprit. In her brother's case, we discovered later it had to do with early childhood programming. On this occasion, the programming wasn't done by parents or other adult authority.

Their family had moved when her brother was in the sixth grade. They had gone from a relatively progressive school district to a rural area where the schools were academically about a year behind. As a result, her brother was able to shoot to the head of his class. Suddenly he was making A's and B's on his report card. He was also one of the best athletes in his class. This was great for her brother's self-image and he started becoming more popular. Before long he began dressing in the latest fashions and was getting quite a bit of attention from girls in the school. He was also getting some attention from the "townies"—local kids who resented this newcomer's success. Three times he was jumped by several of these youngsters. The last one resulted in a brief hospitalization. When discharged, he returned to school and started dressing like everybody else. His grades also dropped to average. Before long he was accepted by the local boys and life settled down to the norm of mediocrity.

Looking back on this experience, her brother indirectly learned something that changed the course of his life. As he explained later, "It's okay to be normal or even a little bit above average. But it's definitely not okay to be excellent. If you do *too* well, something terrible will happen." He had remained mediocre by becoming a binge drinker. He really didn't want a promotion. The negative programming created by the drama of three gang beatings indirectly denied him permission to excel. Lack of permission—an almost superstitious injunction preventing success—and now alcohol all blended together to form a toxic equation. He Elvised out. The Mystery Train was the vehicle.

> *"Put a man in a room where he can play dominoes, read newspapers, and have what he considers good talk, and you'll observe that he will not drink as fast or as deep, or as strongly as he otherwise would. In short, there would be other things to amuse him besides drinking; and what does he drink for, but to amuse himself, and to forget troubles of every kind?"*
> —*Sir Arthur Helps,* Organization in Daily Life

When Curtis returned from Tucumcari, his home near Nashville was only a pit stop. Within hours he was headed for a residential alcohol-treatment center far enough away that he couldn't walk home. He was welcome home but only after graduating from the drug treatment program with the staff's blessing. His family and I chose one of the few programs in the country that could help him. Even though it's a quality program, Curtis still had some legitimate complaints.

"Well, they got me sober. I'll give them that," he chuckled. "But I had a lot more problems than drinking. There was no individual counseling. It was all group work. And there was so much

I just couldn't talk about in a group. And they wanted me to go to AA. Hell! I can't even go to a grocery store without getting harassed. How could I be anonymous at AA? But they never talked about *why* I drink. To me, that was the key. And no one ever touched it."

Most alcoholic and drug treatment centers do exactly what they advertise. They treat alcohol and drug addiction. Drinking, however, in Curtis's case was only a symptom of the problem. The same was true with Elvis. And the same is true of almost all HAPs I've worked with over the years in counseling. They can quit drinking. But the problems continue. They still have to face them, but without benefit of their "medication." So they relapse and begin drinking or using drugs again. That's why the admitted recidivism rate in some treatment programs is as high as eighty percent. Drinking is seldom, if ever, the real problem. In most cases, it's at best a secondary factor.

When I worked in alcohol and drug treatment centers, I discovered it was rare for a person to remain sober after one hospitalization. We always told family members to expect a relapse, and the relapses usually occurred. The fascinating part of this, for me, was most of the staff practiced what they preached. Staff members would end up having relapses. The biggest cause of staff turnover was the counselors' drinking problems resurfacing. In my opinion, they were simply experiencing the same phenomenon. But where I differ from most psychotherapists is how I define it. To me it's not alcoholism or addiction problems. It's the Elvis Syndrome. It's death by success.

Eventually, of course, alcohol abuse becomes a problem independent of the cause. Alcohol is, after all, an addictive drug and the most popular drug in the world today. Continued use of alcohol results in a state of physiological need. The body grows so used to the drug, it must continue to be used for what would be considered normal functioning. As a person grows more tolerant of the drug, more must be used to reach the same feeling of normalcy. You know you're addicted if you develop a craving, or some type of withdrawal symptom when deprived of the drug. As a personal experiment, give up caffeine for a few days. It's a good way to discover the power of addiction. The craving is usually both physical and psychological. The psychological craving can actually go on far longer than the physiological. Since most alcoholics are obsessive-compulsive anyway, they will usually obsess about drinking for years. At AA meetings, you'll hear people who've been sober for decades discussing how much they miss the taste of beer, scotch, or whatever their drug of choice was. That's the power of obsessiveness.

The time it takes to become an alcoholic or drug addict varies from person to person. With some of the more powerful illegal drugs, people can become addicted after one use. With others, it may take ten years or more. The pattern, however, is usually progressive. It begins with periodic-excessive use and then progresses to blackouts or severe memory lapses. Curtis experienced a prolonged blackout when he ended up in Tucumcari. From this point the by-now-serious addict engages in various forms of denial including rationalization, change in drug use pattern, and binges of guilt accompanied by promises to quit. This usually results in increasing and prolonged use, and then either hitting bottom and beginning recovery, or spiraling into a state of hopelessness.

Addiction is serious. But in all cases I've worked with over the years, it's a secondary problem. To solve it, you must treat it as death by success.

"Drunkenness is temporary suicide; the happiness that it brings is merely negative, a momentary cessation of unhappiness."
—*Bertrand Russell,* The Conquest of Happiness

Drug use is not new and not limited to people experiencing the Elvis Syndrome. Opium was apparently used by the Sumarians as early as 5000 B.C. Many South American Indians were chewing coca leaves, the source of cocaine, at approximately the same time. The Chinese distilled alcohol as early as 2000 B.C. American Aztec Indians took ololiuqui, a natural substance similar in structure to the compound we know as LSD, during their religious rites at approximately the same time.

When our own Puritan ancestors lifted anchor to sail to the New World, they left with more beer and wine than water. In fact, the term we use today to measure alcohol content originated from these ancestors. The expression began when gunpowder moistened by the beverage, alcohol was lit. If it exploded, it was "proof" that the beverage contained an adequate amount of alcohol.

Four generations later, Chief Sitting Bull reportedly mixed marijuana with tobacco and passed the peace pipe. The soldiers had already been exposed to marijuana by then. Various kinds of tobacco were chewed during colonial times and after 1810 smoking had become common. During and after the Civil War, wounded soldiers were treated with narcotics. The recently discovered hypodermic syringe made it so easy to administer these pain-relieving drugs that many soldiers became addicted. In fact, for some time, addiction was called the "Army Disease."

At approximately the same time, opium smoking for pleasure began in our country. Chinese workers imported to help construct the railroads brought opium with them. From railroad workers, the practice spread to the underworld. Physicians continued to prescribe morphine generously for various complaints and to allow prescriptions to be filled repeatedly. Others medicated themselves with over-the-counter potions containing morphine, heroin, or cocaine. In fact, cocaine received widespread consumption as an ingredient in Coca-Cola until early in this century. As a result, by the early 1900s an enormous number of Americans were addicted. Finally, in 1914 the government passed legislation to control the manufacture, sale and use of opiates and cocaine. When drugs became illegal, millions of addicts resorted to illegal measures to continue their habit.

It's doubtful any society has ever been as drug-oriented as our own. Drug use is an entrenched part of American culture. Advertising makes drugs appear almost magic. And the magic is consumed regularly. Twenty-seven million pounds of aspirin are consumed per year; one and a half billion drug prescriptions are written each year. According to the National Institute of Drug Abuse (NIDA), Americans now consume well over half the entire world supply of illegal drugs. An estimated twenty-five million Americans smoke marijuana daily. Thirty million people have experimented with cocaine. Over a half million people in our country are known to be heroin addicts. Some thirty million take sedatives, and another twenty million take stimulants on a daily basis.

Eight million Americans chronically abuse tranquilizers. One hundred million consume alcohol regularly, and fifteen percent of those are chronic alcoholics. Another sixteen million smoke approximately two billion cigarettes per day. Over one hundred and twenty million prescriptions are written annually for psychoactive drugs.

Studies show over twelve tons of heroin, sixty-five tons of marijuana, and one hundred and fifty tons of cocaine are consumed throughout the United States annually. The sale of these drugs hauls in over one hundred billion dollars, a figure that exceeds the net sales of General Motors. These numbers are only statistics, but those affected are people. Most of those people are on the Mystery Train, and the next stop is death by success.

> *"First you take a drink, then the drink takes a drink,*
> *then the drink takes you."*
> *—F. Scott Fitzgerald*

It's not necessarily the alcohol or drug abuse that speeds the Mystery Train toward death by success. It's that the alcohol changes the perceptions and ultimate personality of the individual. All of this adds to the impact of The Elvis Syndrome. Fascinatingly enough, this influences not only individuals but also couples and groups as well. One married couple I worked with several years ago, gave a dramatic illustration of this.

They had met their senior year in high school, and began dating soon afterwards. After graduating, they decided to move in together while both were attending college. Several years later marriage followed. They both began ambitious careers and actually got along quite well. They had few problems other than occasional disagreements about money. Within time, however, a tremendous obstacle arose. He got a major opportunity with an expanding company, but there was a hitch. After hiring him, the company decided to enforce a drug-testing policy. They gave employees a ninety-day notice, providing an opportunity to cleanse their systems of any illegal substances. The husband decided he wanted to keep his job, and this is where the problem began.

According to this couple, every night for the past eleven years, they had smoked a marijuana joint together. They would go in their backyard, or sit on the back porch and smoke while relaxing and talking. The ritual began after they graduated from high school and they simply had not stopped. The husband had decided to give up smoking marijuana for his job. He had little difficulty letting go of the habit. He did have backaches and headaches for about ten days and said he occasionally craved it. At someone else's suggestion, he had begun jogging at night during the same time he had previously smoked. This had apparently eased the transition, along with whirlpool and steam baths. He further used his job to motivate himself and was able to accomplish the goal.

But they didn't enter counseling to help him detox from marijuana. They had discovered, to their surprise, they simply didn't like each other absent of marijuana. Since they had quit smoking, they not only argued and had more disagreements, they actually disliked each other. The chronic use of marijuana had altered their personalities and perception over time to the point they were quite compatible. When their marijuana use stopped, however, they didn't enjoy each other at all. They were both very likable people, but their marriage revolved around changes marijuana had produced. They were ultimately faced with the decision of renewing their drug use or ending the relationship. After several visits, the couple agreed to a peaceful but nonetheless painful divorce.

Any psychoactive drug creates a personality change. Curtis's wife has told me a number of stories about him being a "mean drunk." He is one of the most congenial and likable people I have ever known. But I never met him when he was intoxicated. Many years ago, I developed an extremely close relationship with a man who today is a manager for a major corporation. I met him when I was working at a drug treatment center. I was walking down the hall when in my peripheral vision I was shocked to see him soaring toward me. He was flying through a door completely airborne and totally nude. In each hand, he wielded bananas as if they were combat knives. His feet touched down only inches from me. Face to face, nose to nose, he let out a long threatening scream. He was covered with hand-drawn tattoos he'd made with a ballpoint pen. As he screamed, feathers came out of his mouth. It was obvious to me, he was probably experiencing PCP intoxication. I considered him relatively harmless, unless agitated, so I smiled, put my arm around him and entered his room. I noticed his pillow had been shredded, which explained the feathers he exhaled with each breath.

Yet this man was in a responsible job, probably earning twice the amount of money I was. When not using drugs, he was an excellent salesman and later a tremendous administrator. In his case, the drug use resulted from a very self-destructive drive, which is classic among people experiencing the Elvis Syndrome. He has managed to avoid these tendencies over the past several years, and recently was one of the few employees to survive a buyout of his company. He had to give up drug and alcohol use completely. It was a dramatic and dichotomous choice. However, it was worth his career, and more importantly it was worth his life. In his life, the Mystery Train constantly awaited him. It was only through radical intervention and changes that he was able to avoid a rapid death by success.

"Cocaine isn't habit-forming. I should know — I've been using it for years.
— Tallulah Bankhead

Throughout the history of our country, Americans have experienced a love-hate relationship with alcohol. The beverage has held significance in religious rituals, medical practice and dietary use. On the other hand, it has been simultaneously scourged as demonic and evil. In the early history of our country, it was a routine part of everyday life. But those found drunk were placed in stocks for public display and ridicule. Public taverns were not only encouraged, but in some areas required by law. Even with early Pilgrim settlers, the paradox of a love-hate relationship existed. In 1695 a Massachusetts law required a town to be fined if it didn't have a tavern. At the same time the first governor was publicly complaining about drunkenness in his colony.

Today the love-hate relationship continues. Now it's not only with alcohol but with other drugs as well. In Columbia, South Carolina, police raided an ice cream vendor's office. The owner was arrested for selling cocaine from his Mr. Yummy ice cream trucks. In Philadelphia, a dentist was arrested for selling almost six million dollars worth of cocaine per month, primarily to stockbrokers and lawyers. A few weeks later in Houston, a seventy-five-year-old grandmother was arrested and later convicted for selling Valium, codeine, and marijuana from her home.

The drug epidemic is booming nationally and worldwide. And the cost of such abuse is staggering. The price to industry alone from loss of productivity, absenteeism, and accidents is conservatively estimated to be forty-seven billion per year. Drug abusers are three times as likely to be involved in industrial accidents; five times as likely to file worker's compensation claims; and use three times the sick benefits of non-drug users.

Health care expenses exceed those accrued by industry. One study suggested medical costs in the United States due to alcohol use alone exceed one hundred twenty billion per year. Cirrhosis of the liver, resulting almost exclusively from alcoholism, is now the fifth leading cause of death nationwide, surpassing even diabetes. Cirrhosis is the third leading cause of death for both men and women ages twenty-five to sixty-five. If other forms of drug abuse are included, the costs soar to a staggering one hundred ninety billion dollars annually. That figure is more than ten times the government's budget allocated to fight drug abuse.

The cost of drug-related crimes has an additional immeasurable impact. A recent study revealed over half the total criminal suspects tested were using drugs at the time of arrest and over sixty-six per cent had used narcotics the day before their arrest. A University of Chicago study found alcohol and drug use to be directly related to the causes of theft and vandalism among all societal levels. About eighty-two percent of these suspects admitted to taking drugs. Over eighty percent of inmates in federal prisons are serving time because of drug-related arrests.

Drug abuse also takes a high toll from families. Alcoholics are more frequently separated and divorced than non-drinkers and also more likely to be involved in family violence. In one study, well over seventy-five percent of wife abusers in this country had drinking histories. Another report indicated nearly seventy percent of all child abuse cases are alcohol-related. Estimates indicate most rapes and seventy-two percent of criminal assaults are alcohol induced. Most studies of homicides indicate approximately eighty-five percent of all murderers and upwards of half the victims were drinking when the killing occurred.

The costs can also be measured in deaths. Although exact numbers are impossible to obtain, evidence shows more people die from cocaine overdose than from most other medical illness. This does not include the number who die from accidental death, indirectly related to cocaine use. Over half of all traffic fatalities involve alcohol or some other drug. Drugs are involved in upwards of eighty-five percent of all pedestrian fatalities. Sixty-nine percent of all drownings involve drugs as well as sixty-three percent of injuries resulting from falls.

The statistics are alarming. The problem is even more alarming. But those who see this only as a drug problem are missing the point. Yes, alcohol is a drug. All illegal drugs are highly addictive as well. In all the cases you can take away the drugs, but that doesn't solve the problem. The problem is a complex one having to do with the Elvis Syndrome. When we address that issue, then we begin to solve the problem.

"Every form of addiction is bad, no matter whether the narcotic be alcohol or morphine or idealism."
—Carl Jung

The Elvis Syndrome is very nondiscriminatory. It follows an equal-opportunity policy and doesn't differentiate due to race, religion, educational background, or any other basis. Father Tim can testify to that. Tim is one of the best-educated and most intelligent men I know. He was educated in some of the best seminaries and graduate schools in the world. He had earned five different graduate degrees. But all this brilliance didn't prevent his passage on the Mystery Train.

Tim's downfall wasn't unusual. What was remarkable was his

understanding of it. He had a singular insight into his own functioning. But even his brilliance wasn't enough. We had spoken on many occasions. I had conducted several seminars at his church many years ago. Since that time we had spoken personally two or three times per year and over the telephone probably monthly. We had become friends and confidantes. When I had personal trouble, I would often talk to him. On this occasion, he came to see me.

It wasn't shocking when Tim admitted to me he had a severe drinking problem. On the day he came to see me, we chatted superficially for a few minutes. He asked me about my family and how the boys were doing. I inquired about his parents and siblings. We chatted about some of his church members and other friends we had in common. Then Tim became more serious and told me he had come to two conclusions.

"First of all," he said, "I'm addicted to alcohol. I crave it. I think about it all the time. I'm drinking in the morning now. I plan my day around alcohol use. I love it. I worship it. It's my god. And I'm in trouble.

"I know I need to give it up, but I'm scared to. I need to be detoxed, for sure, and maybe even enter a treatment program. I already know that. You don't have to persuade me. You don't have to convince me. I'm a believer.

"But more important—I know how I got here. I know why I drink." He looked up and smiled with a twinkle in his eye. Rather than answering, I nodded, knowing he would continue.

"Did you ever watch *The Twilight Zone* or *The Outer Limits* when you were a kid?" I nodded my head in response. "Do you remember an episode called 'The Sin Eater'?"

I shrugged my shoulders and shook my head, "No, no, I don't remember anything like that at all. I watched *The Twilight Zone* a lot, but I don't remember anything about 'The Sin Eater'."

"Well," he continued, shaking his hand back and forth like it didn't matter. "I don't remember much about it either. But what I do remember had a dramatic impact on me even though I was a teenager. What I do remember is the important thing." He leaned toward me and continued his story more intensely. He squinted his eyes and furrowed his brow.

"See, there's this village. I can't remember where—seems like it was somewhere in Eastern Europe. Anyway, when any of the villagers died, somebody would go get this guy who was called 'The Sin Eater.' He would have to go to the house where the deceased had lived. And it was like the more the dead guy had sinned, the more food the family would cook up. Then 'The Sin Eater' would have to eat all the food. I mean if the guy had sinned very little, it would just be a little bit of food. But if he had sinned a lot, it would be an enormous feast. If I remember correctly, the idea was if 'The Sin Eater' ate all the food, then he would consume the sins of the deceased. The dead person's soul could then be free to travel on into the netherworld, or wherever he was headed.

"As you can imagine, this guy got pretty big. I mean that literally as well as figuratively. He was huge from eating all this food. And as time went by, he got older and then suddenly he got sick and died. His son inherited the responsibility to become 'The Sin Eater.' So the son is notified of his dad's death and he got ready to go there.

"And the drama on the show really builds up at this point. I mean, I can remember thinking—you know—I don't get it. I don't understand what's going to happen here. I didn't know if there was going to be a ghost at the dad's house or what.

"So anyway, the son is shown walking into his father's house. He's the brand new 'Sin Eater.' He opens the door. At first all you see is the son's face. And he's totally shocked! It looks like he is just overwhelmed. And maybe he has seen a ghost or something! You don't know what he sees. But you can tell by his face it's something shocking. It's like a freeze-frame on this kid's face.

"And then after some dramatic music and probably five or six seconds of him turning white and about ready to pass out, the camera very dramatically goes over into the kitchen. There set out on four or five tables are just mountains of food. The tables are just overflowing with food and this boy's got to eat it all. And I guess the message was that his father had absorbed so many of the villagers' sins. It was an incredible number of them. And he hadn't taken time to confess them and get rid of them or whatever. Now his son looks at these tables, totally shocked that he's got to consume all these sins. And then, just like that, the show is over. And I was scared to death!

"Even as a kid, I was blown away. I was shocked by it. And it really struck me—even to the point that today as a I tell this story I'm still overwhelmed by it. But even more dramatic for me is that the show was almost prophetic. Because you see, this is how I feel right now.

"It's exactly how I feel. I feel like *I'm* a 'Sin Eater.' You know what I'm saying? I take care of everybody. I mean my entire parish wants a piece of me. I take care of them. I listen to them. I cater to them. I give to them. I mean, I even live for them. I counsel with them. I work with their kids. I go over to see them when they're sick. It's like I eat their damn sins. I clean up after all their mistakes, but the punch line is, there's nobody to eat *my* sins. So I drink. I drink to relax. I drink to escape. I drink to fight loneliness. Sometimes I just drink to drink.

"But most of all—and I've come to this conclusion slowly over time—I think I drink because I want out. I think I'm exhausted with being a 'Sin Eater'. But I don't have the courage to just walk away from it. You know, it's like that would be the coward's way out. But if I'm an alcoholic, then somehow I didn't give up. I didn't quit. If I'm an alcoholic, maybe they will force me out.

"Now, I know this sounds strange but somehow to me that sounds more noble than just quitting. Do you understand what I'm saying? It's like I'm wounded or killed in action or something. You know. So I'm drinking myself to death so I don't have to resign from my ministry. But the real bottom line—you gotta hear, John—is that I'm tired of being a 'Sin Eater.' I want out of this. I'm successful at what I do, but I'm willing to kill myself to get out of it."

I nodded very slowly and solemnly. We just looked at each other for a few minutes. He had tears in his eyes, and coughed, and then cleared his throat. Finally, with awkwardness, trying to break the silence, he spoke again.

"You want to come over and eat tonight? I fixed up a big plate of spaghetti and some tossed salad and garlic bread. It's lot more than I can eat and . . . ."

We looked up at each other simultaneously and laughed.

Journal Session

1. The St. Louis talk-show brother experienced a traumatic learning in his childhood. This learning had long-range consequences that affected him through adulthood. Virtually everyone has had a similar experience. With some people it's learning a fear of intimacy from an abusive parent. Others may have developed a phobia as a result of some trauma that may have happened in early childhood. Describe one example of traumatic learning that occurred in your childhood that affects you today. How has it hindered your development as an adult?

2. Some people drink as a way of sedating their feelings. Other people eat, have sex, or watch TV. Describe an anxiety-reducing behavior which you engage in. Discuss the long-term consequences of this behavior. Define whether it's possible to find another behavior that will release tension that doesn't have adverse long-term consequences.

3. Describe the drugs you consider yourself addicted to. Remember nicotine, caffeine, and alcohol are drugs. Describe the prices you may pay, either financially or otherwise, for maintaining this addiction. Then describe any severe long-term consequences which could result from continuing the addiction.

4. Describe the prescription drugs you are taking or have taken over an extended period of time. If the drug is mood-altering in nature, take a serious look at a current edition of the *Physician's Desk Reference*. Note the side-effects and discuss them with your personal physician.

Chapter Six Checklist

Directions: Check each statement that applies to you.

___1. Periodically I go on binges of (drinking, eating, dieting, over-exercising, gambling, having sex, etc.) Afterward I feel guilty and vow I'll never do it again.

___2. I have experienced memory loss or blackouts due to drug or alcohol use.

___3. I smoke marijuana occasionally.

___4. I drink to feel relaxed and to unwind from the tension of the day.

___5. I hide no-no's (booze, candy, drugs) in places where my family won't find them.

___6. There are times when I can give up (drugs, tobacco, drinking, over-eating, etc.), but when the tension-level gets too high I can't help myself.

___7. I know I am a highly intelligent person, and it bothers me that I can't control my drinking, or smoking, etc.

___8. I have been through a detoxification program and have had at least one relapse.

___9. I use sleeping pills regularly.

___10. I am taking or have taken prescription mood-altering drugs.

How to Score Yourself: Total the check marks. More than five checks suggest problems with addictions. Use the Writing Session to help you discover the reasons related to the Elvis Syndrome that may be behind your behavior. If you checked number eight, it is especially important to try and determine the pattern of the Elvis Syndrome in your life.

Chapter 7

THE FOOL SUCH AS I
WILL I 'ELVIS OUT'?

"Integrity is so perishable in the summer months of success."
— *Vanessa Redgrave*

"It's not that I don't love her," Ron explained. "I do love her. It's not the same as it was. She's right about that. It's just not. I don't need her any more like I once did. But I do love her. And I don't want to hurt her. I really want to avoid that."

Ron was attempting to explain the evolution of his own Elvis Syndrome. He's not famous. Relatively few people would recognize him, even within his own community. Most who would know him are employed by his father's company and watched Ron grow up. What they saw during his childhood explains what happened years later.

To put it gently, Ron was not a handsome child. I've seen pictures of him from elementary and junior high school. Bluntly, all that stands out in the photographs are knees and nose. His parents were volatile people and didn't waste time attempting to control it. They came from vastly different cultures. His mom was Syrian and his father Chinese. For whatever reason, their marriage worked, if working means remaining together. They definitely worked but not much of anything else. His parents built a company ultimately employing over a hundred people. Ron was raised by company employees, usually wives of supervisors. He was not allowed to participate in sports or other extracurricular activities, primarily because of his size. As a seventeen-year-old high school senior, Ron was five-foot-seven and one hundred twenty six pounds.

After spending a year with his mother's family, Ron entered college. There he met Janie, who later became his wife. She was everything he wasn't. Janie was confident, beautiful, and cunning. In her, Ron saw someone who could make him feel better about himself. And Ron was everything Janie wasn't. He was submissive, compliant, but most of all wealthy. Her beauty legitimized Ron, just as his parents' money legitimized her. She was the first girlfriend he ever had, the first one he ever kissed, and the first girl he ever got pregnant out of wedlock. She was also the first girl who said, "If you don't marry me, I'll sue you and your family." He married her, and things were fine as long as he needed her beauty to feel good about himself.

But eventually Ron grew into his nose. He put on weight, developed his body, and became quite athletic in his late twenties. In addition, he had become president of his parents' company and was considered a business success. Other women began to flirt with him regularly and he soon became promiscuous. Ron's behavior not only led to problems in his marriage but within the company as well. Janie had completely lost control of Ron by this time. He no longer needed her, but she certainly still needed his money. She had lost some of her looks, but she had maintained her cunning.

A long and elaborate series of manipulations transpired before Ron ended up in psychotherapy. He had actually been "caught in the act" with other women on several occasions. His parents were attempting to regain control of the company. His alcohol use had grown to be a major problem, and he was arrested for drunken driving twice within six months. Their corporate bank had refused to extend needed credit recently, which had created massive problems for the company. Ron's attorney had encouraged him to seek marriage counseling, more to delay a nasty divorce that could have created more corporate problems.

Ron is real. His situation is disguised enough to protect his identity. The circumstances actually occurred. At the time I met him, Ron was in stage six of the Elvis Syndrome. Things got a bit worse before they improved. But he did survive. During one of our private discussions, which occurred much later, Ron voiced a valid question. "Why me?" He wondered aloud. "Why did this have to happen to me instead of someone else? Is there something wrong with me that created this?"

Ron's question is one I hear often. The Elvis Syndrome does not happen to everybody and he probably didn't have anything wrong with him that made it occur. The reason he experienced it more intensely than others is explained in this chapter. You can learn from Ron's mistakes or make them yourself. Death by success can be avoided. But you must know how to do it.

> *"If you want knowledge, you must toil for it; if food, you must toil for it;*
> *and if pleasure, you must toil for it: toil is the law."*
> *—Ruskin*

Social network, introduced in chapter one, includes a variety of things. The obvious ones are family, friends, and socialization. During his childhood, Ron's family was either absent or arguing. He was deprived of his mother, who was actually busier building the company than his father was. Due to the stress of building a business, or simply because of clashing personalities, they argued constantly. It increased when they were around. Ron. "I never felt like a child," Ron once commented, more as fact than complaint. "I was a nuisance, or a coincidence or something. But not a child. Hell, I never even was a thought, much less a person." It's difficult to develop confidence or a stable personality in such a setting. Ron married someone much like his mother. Janie was shrewd, manipulative and cunning. She needed money to fulfill her grandiose fantasies. Ron's mother had similar needs. Instead of marrying someone who already had money, she found a man she could manipulate into helping *her* generate it. Ron's marriage was much like his parents'. Those who have a more functional family do stand a better chance of avoiding death by success.

Friends are also a major part of the social network. As indicated in a previous chapter, they can often be the determining factor as to the direction the Elvis Syndrome will take. In summary, friends who add to the isolation or insulation lead the HAP to be "a fool such as I". Those who gently but firmly confront the HAP and hold the mirror of reality up to him or her are more constructive. The HAP doesn't need drinking buddies, yes-men, or groupies. Unfortunately, those are usually the people most attracted to him.

It doesn't take long to realize Elvis had problems in both of these areas. As we have already discussed, his family life left much to be desired. His only friends were employees or groupies. Changes in either of these likely would have resulted in extending his life. Even as an adult, Elvis, or any of us, can expand our social network or create a new family. It's never too late to go back to the basics.

Socialization is also part of the social network. Socialization refers to how the HAP has been prepared to handle success. As a child, Ron had little opportunity to experience success or failure. Neither his parents nor his baby-sitters were willing to escort him to Little League sports or other activities. Their excuse was, "He's too thin . . . too sickly . . . or he might get hurt." As a result, he never had a chance to strike out, hit a home run, or even come up to bat. The same excuse prevented him from participating in school activities. He never remembers even being in a school play, though he must have been at some point.

On the other hand, children involved in extracurricular activities are given an opportunity to achieve and fail regularly. Had Ron been involved in a drama club, he would have experienced being the center of attention and even applauded. If he had participated in band as a child, or chorus, he would have had the opportunity to have similar experiences. In any of these activities, he could have experienced the frenzy of winning and the disappointment of defeat, and learned the sun comes up the next day either way. Life goes on.

Had his parents or anyone else taken the time, they could have discussed what it's like to run a small company. They could have advised him of the challenges, temptations, and opportunities he would face. In Ron's case, however, no socialization occurred. It was not that he wasn't prepared to handle success or failure. He simply wasn't prepared for anything.

I've worked with and interviewed a variety of HAPs over the years. In our studies, close to seventy-eight percent either succeed completely on their own or with only a small degree of help from family or others. Only a minority of people who inherit wealth later achieve significantly on their own. Those who do are more likely to advance to stage six than those who achieve success on their own. The opportunity to personally experience success and failure, especially at an early age, seems to be a major component to avoiding the Elvis Syndrome later. Apparently, wealthy parents are in some way more protective of their children. Or perhaps they are more indulgent. After graduation from college, Ron walked right into an executive position with his father's company. Up to that point, he had never worked a day in his life. Within five years he was a vice president. None of this was a result of merit. Ron admitted to me later he was in no way qualified or competent to run the company. So in reality, he had never achieved on his own.

A major competitor in their industry directed his sons to take another route. He wrote contracts with them during their senior year of high school. When they graduated he considered his financial obligations to them complete. However, he suggested they could make a deal. If they went to college, completed ROTC training, and spent a minimum of three years on active military duty, they would meet their portion of the contract. In return, he would pay their complete college costs. He would also buy them new cars when they graduated. If they wanted, he would give them major positions in his company when they completed active duty. He explained the career path they would follow if they decided to work in his organization. He also defined the opportunities and obligations of achieving top leadership positions. It was all done in a very businesslike manner. Both boys agreed and returned after their military experience to the family business. And neither has approached advanced levels of the Elvis Syndrome. Preparation is very important and apparently experiential preparation—specifically when achieved indirectly—is the most valuable.

"As a tale, so is life: not how long it is, but how good it is, is what matters."
—Seneca

I can tell you in incredible detail exactly where I was, what I was doing, and who I was with the moment I heard President Kennedy had been assassinated. Others who were alive during the attack on Pearl Harbor can, even fifty years later, provide similar detail. Some have similar memories of hearing President Roosevelt had died. There are few events in history people recall with such detailed clarity. In my opinion, you can add another date to that list. Years from now, anybody older than ten in 1994 will be able to tell you in startling detail about Friday night, June 17, 1994. The entire world was hypnotized by the pathetic forty-three mile per hour dirge proceeding down the Los Angeles free-ways like a New Orleans Creole funeral procession. The creoles call it a "second line." The O. J. Simpson story gripped America. The circus and "second lining" following his arrest likely will result in dramatic changes in both American media and the justice system. But the purpose of this discussion is not to analyze or critique the case. Nor is it to assign guilt or innocence. The question is, how did it get to that point? The answer is found in deification. The process introduced in chapter one by MDWIFE.

Deification is a major factor differentiating those who evolve into upper levels of the Elvis Syndrome. Whether deification destroys you or not, has to do with your emotional equipment. The more you are equipped to deal with emotional issues, including fame or media influence, the better off you'll be. Another important factor is how you handle the pressure of being the big fish, regardless of the size of the pond. A third factor is the group, organization, or company you are close to. An additional factor is the length of time your own Elvis Syndrome builds. But the most important consideration is how well you deal with deification.

Deification simply defined, occurs when you consciously or unconsciously begin to think of yourself in any way as godlike. If deification continues, death by success is inevitable without intervention. The primary problem is that deification is not something you sit around and discuss. I've never met a HAP who claimed to be godlike. Deification is a very symbolic and figurative process that normally begins outside of everyday awareness.

Often however, HAPs do begin to believe on some level they're above rules and laws. Some conclude that normal cause-and-effect relationships don't apply to them. This probably explains why HAPs who use drugs so frequently overdose. They consider themselves immune. A chilling and prophetic example of deification was described in the June 27, 1994, issue of *Time* magazine. Police were called to the O. J. and Nicole Simpson residence on New Year's Day, 1989. Nicole came running out of the house in a bra and sweatpants, badly cut and bruised. O. J. appeared a few minutes later and began yelling at the police: "The cops have been here eight times before, and now you're going to arrest me. This is a family matter." O. J. apparently felt impervious to the law. His response implied it was an inconvenience for him to be interrupted. The results speak for themselves.

Anyone placed on a pedestal is put in an unnatural situation. If they remain there long enough, the results can be disastrous. Humans are obviously unable to handle being worshiped. And when deification occurs HAPs soon begin to deteriorate. The list of people who have experienced this is endless. When a HAP begins to think the rules don't apply, he soon finds out otherwise.

Deification is partially a cooperative process. It's actually an interaction between the HAP and others around her. People treat celebrities differently than those who aren't. The deferential treatment they get is part of the problem. And HAPs cooperate in the transaction. Society apparently needs heroes and wants to get close to them. So we buy the shoes or clothes they endorse. We buy videos they narrate. Children begin to dress like HAPs, especially the entertainers or athletes. We elevate them from heroes to icons. Deification develops further as both the HAP and society begin to believe their press clippings. Everyone is hooked at this point. Society needs Roseanne as much as she needs us. And we smile and dance to the mutually destructive beat of a sickeningly familiar tune. She leads and we follow, then we lead and she follows. And when she tires, we will replace her with another. And if it weren't her, we would choose someone else. The demise she may ultimately experience will be a similar cooperative dance. The same is true with O. J. Simpson, Mike Tyson, and Michael Jackson. It is also true of less-celebrated

HAPs such as Jim Bakker, Jimmy Swaggart, and Leona Helmsley. However, after the fact, any of these people would tell you natural laws do apply. Cause-and-effect relationships do affect them. Survivors and family members of the Jonestown massacre and the legacy of David Koresh in Waco, Texas, can assure you of that. And certainly, though deification may be a real phenomenon, people are not deities.

"The Superego is that part of the personality which is soluble in alcohol."
—Professor Harold Lasswell

Cow Pies once gave a penetrating description of media impact on the Elvis Syndrome. "Television," he smiled, "really does make you bigger than life. It creates this recognition that is simply unnatural. You know what I mean? It makes people think you're more important than you really are. And then pretty soon you begin to believe it yourself.

"I mean, people see you on TV and they want to be around you. They think you're a star because you're on television. And probably on a local level that really is the truth. I mean, news anchors are the stars in every small market that has a television station. I don't ever go out when somebody doesn't offer me a free beer, a mixed drink, or something. And you can't win. If you say no, they think you're conceited. If you say yes all the time, before long you're a damn drunk." He laughed and shook his head while rubbing his left temple. I nodded my head in agreement and smiled. He seemed to be experiencing a pressure to speak, so I dared not interrupt.

"It's really strange. I have personally been offered—for free by the way—cocaine, uppers, downers, sex with women, sex with men, everything you can think of. There was even this one guy who, honest to God, tried to get me to sleep with his wife for her birthday!" He leaned toward me for emphasis as his eyes grew more intense. "For money!"

I laughed out loud with him and shook my head. "That's a first." I continued laughing. "I've never heard of giving your wife *that* for a birthday present!" The anchorman shook his head back and forth as he rubbed his palms together.

"The worst thing at all, at least for me, is that people think that because you're on TV you must be rich. And you know how bizarre that is. The number one anchor in a market this size *might* make $25,000 a year. But people think you make a lot more than that. And you end up wanting to perpetuate this image. See. It's like the image becomes more important than reality. And you spend all this money to feed the image.

"Personally, I couldn't survive without credit cards. And I don't know anyone in the business who could. So you get more in debt and more in trouble. Once a month I used to pay my bills. And I'd always get real upset after I was done because I had to face how far behind I was. So I'd get all depressed and go buy some liquor and charge it on my Visa! I'd just make the problem worse by charging more, when that's what I was upset about to begin with. Can you believe that? It made my drinking problem and my debt problem worse automatically."

The influence of media is overwhelming. You only have to look at who society's heroes are today to realize the power of television, newspapers, and movies. With increasing media exposure, the probability of the Elvis Syndrome soars. O. J. Simpson once again provides an example. The public first watched him on television as one of the most prolific runners in the history of college football. We smiled and nodded our heads in agreement as he won the Heisman trophy and continued to applaud as he played professional football. He hypnotized us with his running ability. We were entertained and even envious. We later watched him as an actor, sports announcer, and in commercials. And we laughed incredibly as he even parodied himself in the *Naked Gun* movie series. "Juice" most definitely became bigger than life and was deified as a result. He was placed on a pedestal and worshiped. And he didn't have the emotional equipment to handle any of it. To whatever degree, his self-image became supernatural. And as with all cases of deification, if you are supernatural the natural laws don't apply.

In the 911 police call recording made public weeks after his arrest, O. J. screamed, "You can't treat O.J. like that! You can't do that to O.J.!" He referred to himself in the third person. Apparently, in his own eyes, he was beyond being a person. He was bigger than "me" or "I." He didn't perceive himself as an individual. He was an institution, or a deity, to himself and obviously to others. The mob crowding along the Los Angeles highways and the media coverage of the O. J. caravan the night of his arrest is proof enough. The Stanford University Band even preformed outside the courtroom during jury selection.

When a HAP begins to receive a great deal of media focus, the likelihood of deification soars. The emotional equipment required to handle such focus is almost never in place. From a small-town TV anchorman to a national icon like O. J., media exposure can propel you toward death by success, but it doesn't necessarily have to be.

> *"There is perhaps no one of our natural passions so hard to subdue as*
> *Pride. Disguise it, struggle with it, beat it down, stifle it as much as one*
> *pleases, it is still alive, and will every now and then peep out . . . .*
> *For even if I could conceive that I had completely overcome it,*
> *I should probably be proud of my humility."*
> *—Benjamin Franklin*

In 1956 Dwight Eisenhower was president. There were no Japanese cars in the United States. And Elvis Presley was twenty-one years old. One Saturday night, early in the year, Elvis stared at a camera and slurred, "Ladies and Gentlemen, I would like to do a song now that tells a little story that really makes a lot of sense. 'Awop bop a lo bop—a lop ban boom! Tutti frutti! All rooti! . . ." It was the shot heard 'round the world and probably the beginning of the first Elvis Syndrome. Television pulled the trigger. Yet death by success can occur without television at all. Media influences simply expedite it. It's not TV that's the problem. There was no TV for Fitzgerald, Hemingway, or Van Gogh. The challenge is how you as an individual handle attention, success, and fame. Whether you get television, radio, or newspaper exposure is irrelevant. Success and notoriety are the critical factors. Being the "big fish in a small pond" is actually far worse than being a "big fish in a big pond." This is true because in big ponds there will be other "big fish." The fame is diffused. Additionally, in a small pond there is less opportunity for review of leadership. Large corporations, as an example, have stock-holders, boards, and management assessments to hopefully deter such problems. But in small organizations, little if any such help is possible.

An extreme case of this is found with entertainers or perform-ers. They are, in essence, small businesses, and the performer is the product. Though he or she may have staffs to assist, it is usu-ally a one-man or one-woman show. The performer is not only the big fish but in many cases the pond. If staff members were to discuss what they perceived as self-destructive behavior, they would probably risk getting fired. These are also the cases where deification and media exposure are most likely to become a risk.

In the past, writers and philosophers were the ones who had trouble with self-sabotage. They were the personalities of their day in the absence of television, radio, and the silver screen. Equally self-destructive were the musicians of that era. These performers were the personalities. Hemingway and Fitzgerald were the Michael Jacksons and Anthony Hopkinses of their time. And in their cases, they were also the big fish who owned the pond. The history of death by success with this group of peo-ple was phenomenal. Recently their genre has been replaced by athletes, entertainers, and actors. Yet the self-destructiveness continues, and for the same reason.

It's rare to hear of someone in a position such as the president of General Motors, Ford, or General Electric going through the same kind of problems we've discussed with others who experi-ence the Elvis Syndrome. They have to respond to board reviews, staff psychologists, stockholders, as well as senior exec-utives who don't necessarily fear them. Similarly, it's very rare for a high-ranking military officer to experience the Elvis Syndrome. Accountability is just too great, both from the top and bottom. Even at the highest levels, there is always someone hold-ing you accountable. In smaller organizations, however, this isn't true. The big fish in the big pond has people watching him or her. The big fish in the small pond is given too much opportunity to self-destruct. This applies to people working within these compa-nies. But it also applies to the companies themselves. Companies can actually Elvis out as well.

*"Every institution not only carries within it the seeds of its own dissolution,
but prepares the way for its most hated rival."*
— *William Ralph Inge*

In 1985 Cabbage Patch dolls earned approximately six hundred million dollars in sales. The next year, they lost one hundred eleven million dollars. On July 18, 1988, the parent company filed for bankruptcy. In reorganization, they went from twenty-five hundred employees to seven hundred. Near the same time every child wanted an Atari video game. Today, Atari is no longer a factor in the video game market place. Wang Laboratories with their mini computers revolutionized office procedures for the entire world. At its peak, Wang employed thirteen thousand workers. In August 1992, Wang announced it would file Chapter Eleven bankruptcy. On July 22, 1992, Phar-Mor founder, Mickey Monus, opened his three hundredth store and promised there would be three hundred more. Two days later the dismantling of Phar-Mor began. In ten years it grew to a three-billion-dollar business. Monus eventually faced 129 counts of fraud. The June 29, 1994 *Wall Street Journal* followed up on the Phar-Mor case. It claims the federal authorities are investigating whether jury tampering by Monus by two of his supporters and former employees caused the deadlock in his trial. The Elvis Syndrome is not limited to people. Organizations go through it. And it probably occurs daily.

The evolution of death by success in a corporation is not that different than it is with a person. Elvis's self-sabotage took the following steps:

Step One	Elvis unknown truck driver and amateur musician.
Step Two	Records two songs for mother and several months later given an opportunity for professional recording
Step Three	Begins touring after release of "That's All Right, Mama."
Step Four	Meets Colonel Tom Parker and period of expansiveness begins.

Step Five	Exponential success followed by increased insulation and isolation.
Step Six	Death by success begins with increased emotional problems, drug abuse, and difficulties.
Step Seven	Death.

A small corporation I consulted with recently followed a similar pattern:

Step One	Company founder unknown employee of another company.
Step Two	Discusses idea for a new company with two other people.
Step Three	Major investor located and partnership is formed.
Step Four	Company begins to experience rapid and expansive success.
Step Five	Major growth. Company triples in size. Partners become isolated from workers and customers due to rapid period of growth.
Step Six	Death by success begins due to founder's lack of contact with customer base and employees.
Step Seven	Company bought out at loss after entering Chapter Eleven.

Another small company followed a similar pattern, but step six began when the founder's son, who was vice president of marketing, became addicted to cocaine and alcohol. He began making erratic decisions while under the influence and lost two major accounts. Ultimately this led to the downfall of the company.

Although it's difficult to do so without any personal information, a look at the reported death by success of Phar-Mor demonstrates a similar pattern:

| Step One | Founder Mickey Monus works in family business. |
| Step Two | He and friend decide to enter discount drugstore business. |

Step Three	Financing acquired and chain begins.
Step Four	Chain begins growing. Within ten years two hundred plus stores opened.
Step Five	Phar-Mor expands into lines that violate its own policies. Monus invests in semipro basketball and Major League baseball teams. Becomes preoccupied.
Step Six	Monus isolates himself, associating exclusively with professional athletes. Marries younger woman. Death by success begins as Monus grows more insulated. Later accused of embezzling ten million dollars.
Step Seven	Phar-Mor chain reorganizes.

You can trace the same steps with personalities such as Donald Trump, John DeLorean, Michael Milken, John Gutfreund and dozens of others. Corporations are simply composed of people. Therefore the same fundamental principles apply. In the same way, similar remedies will work. To reduce the threat of a company experiencing the Elvis Syndrome, you strengthen the social network and emotional equipment.

I consulted with a highly successful small company that was bought out by a Fortune 500 corporation. The small company had been founded and built by a workaholic, hands-on, hypermaniac. He's an incredible man who literally built the organization from an idea to the point where it was purchased. His leadership style was personal, visceral, and homespun. And his employees loved it. He knew each of them personally, cared about their families, and even began a scholarship program for children of his employees. He was dynamic and aggressive, but never too busy to help someone in trouble. But when he sold the company, employees felt betrayed. The void left by the founder was filled by a collective mourning and sense of loss and depression. The new CEO was an equally dynamic and personable individual, but he couldn't fill the founder's shoes. He was astute enough to begin strengthening the social network.

We began by having small-group meetings with management. The goal was to provide employees an opportunity to safely discuss their feelings about the purchase. They knew nothing about it until it happened. They didn't even have an opportunity to say goodbye to the founder. They feared losing their jobs and were filled with sadness, anger, betrayal, and insecurity. Our first strategy was to strengthen the employees' emotional equipment. After completing the sessions with management, I trained them to implement similar small-group meetings with employees. This accomplished two goals: It helped strengthen the employees' emotional equipment and expanded the social network opportunities throughout the company.

The founder had created a family. He was the dad and Dad had left Mom and abandoned his family. Dealing with these feelings hundreds of times in psychotherapy has taught me their power. The new CEO could never be Dad. But he could be a benevolent stepfather and friend. As in any other situation like this, the employees needed to be reassured he cared. This would have to be repeated redundantly.

The company reintroduced complaint boxes, suggestion boxes, and employee-oriented newsletters. Then we constructed multiple bulletin boards and began an employee day-care center. Next we set up an employee counseling program and started softball, basketball and volleyball teams. Ultimately we convinced the parent corporation to allow the founder to return. We gave him a surprise going-away party. Afterward each employee was given the opportunity to look him in the eye, shake his hand, and say goodbye. The employees still miss the founder. The guy's a real "hoot." There will never be another like him. But this company is not going to experience death by success. They introduced enough strategies to avoid it.

"Even victors are by victory undone."
—John Dryden

Steven Seagal, in *Marked for Death*, stoically described to a friend, the results of a recent confrontation. Though it's probably not a direct quotation, Seagal said, "One thought he was invincible. The other thought he could fly."

"Well?" his friend asked. "What happened?"

"They were both wrong." Seagal deadpans.

Of course Seagal had shot one and thrown the other out a twentieth floor window.

About the time you think you're invincible, something happens to convince you otherwise. In actuality, the sooner you find out you're not invincible, the better. Considering all that HAPs go through and the potential consequences, it's best discovered early. Curtis pointed this out in a telephone conversation shortly before this book was completed. We'd been discussing the incredible increase in the number of people experiencing the Elvis Syndrome.

"Yeah, I think you're right with that deity complex thing," Curtis suggested. "Damn, it's a powerful process. I think the younger you are, the worse you get hit."

"That's probably true," I responded. "And probably the longer you go before you deal with deification, the harder it is too."

"Now, what?" Curtis laughed. "Did you say the longer you go without *defecation*, the harder it is? Is that what you said?"

I joined him laughing. "No, Crazy." I joked. "*Defecation* is what you're full of. I'm talking about 'd-e-i-f-i-c-a-t-i-o-n! Like you said earlier, the deity complex."

"I know," he chuckled. "I was just teasing you. Actually, you and I both are full of defecation. That's another problem." Curtis laughed aloud. "I think you're right on target. At least with my career it's been like that. The fans are great. Live concerts are head trips for musicians. You were backstage! You saw it, right?"

"Well," I paused. "I observed it. I sure didn't experience it like you all did. But, yeah, it's got to be a mess. I don't know how anybody could handle that kind of focus."

"Man, you're right." Curtis assured me. "I just don't think anybody could without getting a little crazy before too long. We gotta keep it in perspective here, that we're people, not idols. Not gods or heroes. We're just singers. We're just people who can play music. But it's damn easy to get confused. You get deceived into thinking you're invincible. And you do it to yourself. Your fans do it to you. And you go on and on. But listen to this . . . .

"You know who's got this worse than anybody? Judges. There's a guy in our church who's a damn judge. Now I've known this guy since he was in kindergarten and I've watched him go through it all. This SOB has got it bad. Think about it: the robe, sitting up higher than anyone else, everyone standing when you come in and go out, being called "your honor" instead of Billy—even the whole idea of passing judgement. Now that's deification!"

"Wow!" I exclaimed. "I never thought about that. But man, you're right. They would get a bad case of it."

"Well, this jerk's definitely got it." Curtis paused momentarily. "By the way, you think this was really what happened with O.J.?"

"I don't know," I shook my head. "I don't know. I guess all of it came together in his situation. The media, deification, the whole process. There were definitely no winners in that story. I'm telling you, in that one nobody won."

As with other conversations I've had with Curtis, this one brought out one of the biggest tragedies of the Elvis Syndrome. It's neither a win-win nor win-lose proposition. In all cases, it's lose-lose. Everybody loses. When Elvis died, everyone lost. And in every case since then, the same scenario is repeated. Death by success benefits no one. There are only losers. The only way to win is to avoid it.

JOURNAL SESSION

1. People get married for a variety of reasons. Frankly, the reasons are usually "bad." In fact, the younger you married the more likely the reasons were unhealthy. In the case of the couple mentioned in the beginning of the chapter, the reasons for marriage were defined in detail. In a similar way, choose your current marriage or any other relationship you've been involved in previously. Look for the real reasons you entered that relationship. Be honest with yourself. Also realize simply because you entered a relationship for an unhealthy reason does not mean you need to get out of that relationship today.

2. Describe what your social network is at this point. Look at the various components of your social network including family, friends, workplace, church groups, etc. If you feel your social network is too limited, describe ways you can expand it or make it more healthy.

3. Describe in precise detail where you were, what you were doing, whom you were with etc., the moment you heard President Kennedy was assassinated, or during a similarly momentous event. Then do the same thing for the night you heard or saw the June 17, 1994, caravan of O.J. Simpson.

4. Describe a time when you have been "big fish," regardless of the size of the pond. Give an example of one occasion when you handled the fame well. Then give another example of a time when you did not do as well. What were the results and consequences of each occasion?

CHECKLIST

Directions: Check each one that applies.

___1.   I have inherited or have been promised that I would inherit the family business or substantial family wealth.

___2.   I am employed or have been employed in a family-owned business.

___3.   I could be considered a "big fish" in the organization where I work. This includes my job, church, or service organization.

___4.   Whatever the reason, I did not participate in sports when I was young.

___5.   My parents did not encourage me to participate in extracurricular school activities.

___6.   The first time I was employed was after I graduated from college.

___7.   I am the head of a small company, department, or organization.

___8.   I married for the first time before age twenty-three.

___9. At the time of my marriage, I was living at home.

___10. I do not feel I handle fame well.

___   Total

How to Score Yourself: Total the number of check marks. The higher the number the greater your risk for the Elvis Syndrome. Scores greater than five suggest difficulties in the area of not being given the opportunity to struggle. Review the written material for suggestions for help in this area.

Chapter 8

DREAM OF A BETTER LAND
BALANCE IN LIFE

"First our pleasures die—and then our hopes, and then our fears, and when these are dead, the debt is due. Dust claims dust, and we die too.
—Percy Bysshe Shelley, Death

C urtis once told me about the last time he saw Elvis personally. Curtis said he had been at Graceland visiting one of the King's staff members. By this time, Elvis had become more eccentric and withdrawn from virtually everyone but the few members of his inner circle. His obesity had become a subject of curiosity and gossip among musicians and people associated with the industry. Curtis said he hadn't gotten close enough to speak to Elvis, and didn't even know if Elvis would have remembered him.

"Have you ever seen one of those polar bears in the zoo? They just swim back and forth in one of those small pools. Or one of the bears in a cage pacing side to side in kind of a rhythm? You know what I'm talking about?" He asked.

I nodded my head, recalling my last trip to the Atlanta Zoo. I remembered feeling sorry for the polar bear trying to survive in the Atlanta heat and humidity.

"That's what Elvis reminded me of that time," Curtis continued. "I was getting ready to leave Graceland. On the way out, I looked down toward the swimming pool. There was Elvis dressed in a solid white jumpsuit riding a motorcycle around the pool. Just circling around the pool, going nowhere. All alone. Like a big old polar bear pacing around and around and around.

I got completely sick just looking at him. I remember thinking, 'He's lost it. He has totally lost it!' Just like those polar bears! Confined in a small ice-water pool and completely stir-crazy."

It's a pathetic picture Curtis painted, but not surprising. Elvis may have "dreamed of a better land," but the land he lived in the last few years had become an emotional prison. Visualizing him circling the pool repetitively is easy for me. I've seen dozens of people involved in similar ritualistic behavior over the years, primarily in psychiatric hospitals. It's a major part of many obsessive-compulsive disorders. And, as pointed out earlier, Elvis was exceptionally obsessive-compulsive.

Virtually everything he did was overstatement. Elvis did nothing in moderation. His entire life was an exercise in excess. From small things such as his haircut in the early years to his drug use toward the end, he was the King of Excess. His tours, the outfits he wore while performing, even the way he pursued karate are indications of his compulsive nature. The stories of how he gave gifts, purchasing several Cadillacs or a dozen motorcycles all at the same time, express the same tendencies. The most obvious and visible characteristic, however, was his weight gain. The eating pattern described by Curtis in Chapter One obviously contributed to the dramatic change in weight the King experienced.

Virtually all HAPs are obsessive-compulsives. Like Elvis, most are also prone to excess. They become almost humorous at times, and if it weren't so frightening, there are times I'd laugh out loud. A fully wired HAP has difficulty sitting still. The symptoms discussed in Chapter Three include a high level of kinetic activity. In our office we see this daily. Occasionally HAPs will be so hyper that I suggest we take a walk outside. Hopefully, they will expend some nervous energy and settle down. Often, the walk turns into a foot race. It apparently becomes very important for them to win—even a brief walk.

There are other times I encourage HAPs to become involved in exercise programs as a way of leveling out their lives. On one occasion, a thirty-seven year old sales representative returned for her next session highly motivated after this recommendation. She had purchased a two-hundred-dollar pair of running shoes, an even more expensive warm-up suit, and a matching gym bag that had cost well over two hundred dollars. She had jogged three times for a total of three and a half miles. Earlier in the day, before our appointment, she had made reservations to run the first Disneyworld Marathon in Orlando, which was less than three months away. This is a woman who had never been an athlete or had even jogged before my recommendation, and now she planned to run more than twenty-six miles less than twelve weeks later. That's not dreaming of a better land. It's compulsive and it's excessive.

On another occasion, I made a similar recommendation to another HAP. He was quite overweight and decided it was a good way to take care of his obesity. He immediately set some unachievable weight-loss goals against my wishes. I preached to him about the importance of going about this in a leisurely and relaxing way. "Don't make a contest out of this," I exhorted.

A week later LA and I saw him at one of our favorite walking areas. He looked like "The Little Engine That Could," chugging down the road, his back arched almost convexly. His arms and legs gyrated feverishly back and forth in short, chopping motions. He breathed in equally shallow and rapid fashion, and placed one hand up at his neck, checking his pulse while looking at his watch. After recognizing us, he said, "Hi!" and boasted he'd taken thirty seconds off his previous time and increased his pulse rate fifteen beats per minute. He'd made a contest not only out of his run, but his pulse rate as well.

I've seen the same thing happen with tennis, golf, and fishing. A HAP can convert anything into a competition. This obviously removes the therapeutic and relaxing component of any activity suggested as a way of diverting the HAP's obsessiveness. Brian Wilson of Beach Boys fame even took psychotherapy to an extreme. He entered therapy to such excess that he now has a live-in therapist. Incidentally this therapist has also become his manager, agent, and his only friend. (His therapist's fee is a meager fifty percent of all Brian's earnings.) Writer David Felton of *Rolling Stone* magazine made a point about people recovering from addictions. He said there were many definitions of a higher power in twelve-step programs. But he'd never heard of a higher power demanding fifty percent of the gross! Yet fifty percent is not the price of the higher power. It is the price of Brian's obsessiveness.

"There is a certain relief in change, even though it be from bad to worse; as I have found in traveling in a stagecoach, that it is often a comfort to shift one's position and be bruised in a new place."
— *Washington Irving*, Tales of a Traveller

One of the major influences in my life was my grandfather. He was ideally suited for the role, especially in my case. He was extremely patient and the most altruistically nurturing person I've ever met. He taught me much in my life and is predominantly responsible for my own parenting style today. The best thing about Grandpa was that he constantly taught me, but never directly. I can't ever recall him discussing anything by saying, "Let's sit down and talk about . . . ."

His teaching was indirect, conversational, and profoundly effective. On one occasion we had traveled to eastern North Carolina not far from the Atlantic coast. He stopped alongside the road, jumped out of the truck, and told me to follow him. The ground was marshland and swampy. He followed a path and then knelt over, sorting through some of the vegetation. Finally, he spotted what he'd been looking for.

"See that, Johnny?" he pointed to a plant I'd never seen before. "See that?" He reached down, separated the growth, and pointed out a particular plant to me.

"Yeah," I gasped. "What is that? Are those briars or somethin'? What is that?"

"No," he laughed. "Those aren't briars. Those are just part of the plant. That, Son, is a Venus flytrap. It's a man-eating plant!"

"A what?" I asked. "A man-eating plant?!"

Grandpa laughed again. "No, Son. It doesn't really eat men. It eats women!" He guffawed at my reaction and punched me in the arm. "Son, that's a Venus flytrap. It eats flies, bugs, mosquitoes, or anything that's unlucky enough to crawl in that little mouth. Watch this." He took a weed and rubbed it over the inside of the trap. The trap closed quickly like a tight clam shell.

"Wow!" I exclaimed. "That's strange! Let's take it home." I'd never seen anything like that and was quite amazed.

"Can't take it home." He shook his head. "It would die there. The soil's too balanced at home."

"What do you mean?" I asked.

"Well, the reason this Venus flytrap grows this way is that there's not enough nitrogen in the soil," Grandpa explained. "Here the soil's too damp. So this plant gets its nitrogen from flies or bugs or chiggers. It grows here but it won't grow at home. Now, this doesn't look like any other plant you've ever seen, does it?"

"No," I shook my head. "No, no. I've never seen anything like this before."

"Well, that's what happens when you get out of balance. A little sun, a little water, and good soil and you have a good plant. Take any of those away and things don't turn out right. And it's the same way with people. Always stay balanced." He looked toward me. "It's a holy word."

I didn't understand what Grandpa was trying to tell me at the time. However, I'm beginning to understand more and more today. Balance is vital for health. And when a lack of balance exists, there will always be perversion. Obsessiveness is the opposite of balance. The Venus flytrap obsesses about nitrogen. In its lacking, it evolved into a highly unusual plant that can survive only within a particular environment. The same is true of people who become obsessed. They're unable to adapt to the changing world and fear losing control. As a result, many become control freaks and end up obsessing even more. The only antidote I've discovered is balance.

"You only lose energy when life becomes dull in your mind. You don't have to be tired and bored. Get interested in something. Get absolutely enthralled in something. Throw yourself into it with abandon."
—Norman Vincent Peale

Though it's probably not the intent of the original authors, I define Type A personality as achievement-driven. The Type A is propelled by a desire to achieve on some level, external to himself or herself. Achievement becomes not only the goal, but the object of the Type A's obsession. The Type A is obsessed with achievement like the Venus flytrap is obsessed with nitrogen. He or she ignores most other of life's elements and soon the personality begins to resemble that of a Venus flytrap. It's aggressive, obsessed, and perverted. Type B personalities are driven by balance. That also is probably not the original authors' intent, but for the purpose of *The Elvis Syndrome*, that's how the types will be defined. Type B personalities do achieve and over the course of life achieve far more than Type A's. Type B's may not be "as fast out of the gate" as the Type A. But they don't burn out or self-destruct as frequently either.

Type B's don't seem to experience the perpetual sense of urgency Type A's do. And they certainly don't have the health problems of Type A's discussed in Chapter Two. Type B's more likely respond to what's actually important instead of urgent. And they're able to distinguish between the two. The Type B is also able to establish boundaries and assert himself or herself in a non-threatening way. The Type A does these things rarely, if ever, and spends his life reacting and responding.

A personal boundary is an invisible line drawn between self and others. On your side of the boundary are things that are your responsibility. Those on the other side are the responsibility of others. It's important that boundaries be clear. The Type A has difficulty delegating responsibility, simply because his boundaries are vague. So he ends up doing unnecessary tasks quite urgently and attacking others instead of asserting his boundaries. Type B's, on the other hand, driven by balance, assert their boundaries and accept personal responsibility but not the responsibilities of others.

These skills are internal, not external. There is nothing out there directing the Type B where to draw boundaries or when to assert himself or herself. The Type A, on the other hand, is always striving for something. She's motivated by achieving a goal outside of herself. The external focus leads to work as a means of achieving money, status, and things. Type B's internal focus results in enjoying labor for its own sake. The external focus is more filled by what you lack or what you're trying to avoid. Many Type A's fear loss of money, status, or identity so they work harder. But they also work more anxiously. On many occasions the anxiety alone can lead to self sabotage. MDWIFE and Topanga Jack, mentioned in previous chapters, are other examples of what happens when a person is focused exclusively on the external. Topanga Jack was looking for success. He committed all his time and energy to achieving success and all the things that surrounded it. When he accomplished what he'd set out to, he was like a dog who had finally caught the car. He had it but was not sure what to do with it. In Topanga Jack's case the questions he actually asked say more than anything I could create.

"If I'm so damn successful, then why am I miserable?" It's a profound question.

The answer is not necessarily profound but it is accurate. Focusing on success is being driven by achievement. It's looking for *things*. It's obsessing about money, house, and car and ignoring what's really important. Focusing on happiness is different than focusing on success. It's thinking about balance, and looking inside yourself to determine the difference between happiness and achievement. Topanga Jack was asking the wrong question. His goal was happiness, but he asked, "What will make me successful?" He never asked what would make him happy. He was driven by achievement and not balance.

Type A's who are highly obsessive-compulsive can learn to change. They can become more balanced. It takes time and work to accomplish the change but it's well worth the effort. As a consultant, I have found only one way to help these people make dramatic shifts in personality. I attempt to help them focus their tremendous obsessive-compulsive energy toward balance. "Get obsessed with health," I suggest. "Become compulsively balanced." I show them the objective, scientific benefits and at times actually calculate in concrete terms the increase in life expectancy and potential income. One lady pulled out her day planner and asked me to schedule what a balanced day or week would look like. I did, and she started living it. She even scheduled relaxation time, and sex with her husband! She remained obsessive compulsive, but was able to develop Type B traits and improved her life. She used her own obsessive energy to turn her life around rather than to destroy herself.

"I strongly believe that when the natural time is up writers actually do run out of material."
—*Brian Wilson (The Beach Boys)*

I looked out from the rustic front porch. Summer afternoon clouds surged rapidly together like high tide during a Gulf storm. Skies darkened and a soft breeze stirred the August heat. The wooden rocking chairs were faded by years of exposure and use. My rocker creaked and scraped rhythmically against the wooden floor as I turned, smiling at Nanny.

Her tan skin contrasted dramatically with her snowy white hair. She sat in a rocking chair and held a patch for a quilt she was stitching. A thimble covered the tip of her middle finger. Three additional stitching needles were inserted on the left collar of her dress. She wore them like military medals. She held the quilt patch close to her face—almost to her nose—so her aged eyes could see it. Her withered fingers moved rapidly as she stitched in a cadence—one, two, three, pull . . . .

"So why do you always do that?" I asked.

"Do what, Son?" she answered without looking up. One, two, three, pull. One, two, three, pull . . . .

"Why do you always make one patch different from the others?" I asked smiling as she continued.

"Well," she shrugged. "That's just the way you're supposed to do it, Johnny." One, two, three, pull . . . . "You always have to do one patch with a different color thread or off-color. It's got to be different from the rest or it's bad luck. With some patterns, you can even put it upside down or inside out. But you gotta do it." One, two, three, pull . . . .

"Bad luck?" I stopped rocking and leaned over. "I don't get it. How's it bad luck, Nanny?"

She looked up and made eye contact with me. "It's just bad luck, Johnny. Some things are just like that." She continued stitching . . . one—two—three—pull.

"Where did you learn that?" I asked. "I mean, where did you hear that it was bad luck to have everything perfect? Isn't that what you're really saying? That it's bad luck to have a perfect quilt? Where did you hear that?"

"Oh, Lordy," she sighed. "Law! Law! Law! I don't remember, Johnny. I really don't remember. That's just the way you're supposed to do it. It's bad luck to have a perfect quilt! Something bad will happen to you if your quilt's perfect, so you always put in a mistake. But it's not really mistake because you're doing it on purpose." Nanny gazed out as a soft drizzling rain began to tap a light beat on the porch roof.

"It's gonna rain, Son." She smiled and placed the patch back in her basket. "Help Nanny take the chairs in so they don't get soaked." I helped her up and took the chairs in the hallway where she left them when it rained.

"Well, I guess I'd better get on home before it gets too bad." I smiled.

"Oh. Okay, Son." she smiled. "Lean down and give Nanny a hug before you leave." I leaned over and embraced her, avoiding the needles on her collar as I'd learned to do years ago.

Actually, Nanny is not far off the mark. A strong belief has long been held that it's bad luck to do things too well. Certainly there are prohibitions against being perfect dating far back in history. The Roman tradition discussed earlier was based on a superstitious belief about success. The Romans believed if you succeeded too well, you were mocking the gods and would be punished. A similar belief is found in various Asian cultures and throughout various aboriginal groups throughout the world, including several Native American tribes.

George Bernard Shaw and his wife once attended a performance by concert pianist Jascha Heifetz. Afterward, Shaw wrote Heifetz, commending him in a peculiar way. "If you continue to play with such beauty, you will certainly die young," Shaw warned. "No one can play with such perfection without provoking the jealousy of the gods. I earnestly implore you to play something badly every night before going to bed." There are tremendous fears and superstitions surrounding success. Nanny's belief that a perfect quilt is bad luck, the Roman superstition, and Shaw's cautious compliments of Heifetz are all examples of this. But there are more.

Some people have a fatalistic reaction to success. Many of these people have a deep-rooted belief they're alive for a reason. Once that reason is completed, their purpose for existence is gone. For some of these people, achievement has serious and long-term consequences. Procrastination, for these people, is a life-and-death matter and they avoid achieving by whatever means necessary. If you die after you reach your goal, in their opinion, it's best not to reach the goal! Some people avoid completing or taking on projects altogether. To complete it is to die.

Others face additional obstacles. They have a deep-seated belief there is only one big success inside of them. They have been led to fear that once that success is achieved, they'll never be able to repeat it again. This can lead to the ultimate obstacle to success: They commit suicide after achieving notoriety. People shake their heads and say, "Why? He had it all!" But that's precisely the point. He did have it all. And, in his opinion, he'd never have that opportunity again. That was F. Scott Fitzgerald's death by success. It sprang from a belief that there is a limited supply or limited opportunity to succeed.

> *"The secret of happiness is this: Let your interests be as wide as possible,*
> *and let your reactions to the things and persons that interest you be as far*
> *as possible friendly rather than hostile."*
> *—Bertrand Russell*

Elvis sang. Tyson boxed. Richard Nixon politicked. It's fairly easy to identify their obsessiveness. This is not to say these men didn't have other interests. Clearly, they did. Among other things, Elvis studied karate, rode motorcycles, and collected police badges. But when doing these things, he buried himself in them briefly and then went on to something else. When he studied karate, the instructor actually moved to Graceland and was a part of Elvis's entourage. When he focused on motorcycles, Elvis bought a dozen of them. When his energy turned toward police badges, he visited the White House and played secret agent. That's not balance.

The Type A obsessive-compulsive HAP often lives and works in a frenzy. Her pace is unnatural and if you observe closely you may get a queasy feeling something is not quite right. She may work on a project for three days straight with little or no sleep. She may go out dancing every night for weeks on end. She may work all day at the office, come home and clean 'til 3:00 a.m. Then she'll go to bed, get up, and start it all over at six the next morning. One mother asked about her daughter recently, "What, in God's name, is that girl running from?" She is running. And she's running from something. But it's nothing visible. Nobody's chasing her. She's running from one of the few places she probably rarely looks. It's inside her. She's running from her own internal fear. HAPs are driven by achievement. But they're fueled by fear. It can be fear of anything. Some of the most common are: fear of failure; mediocrity; not being _____ enough (fill in the blank: good/smart/attractive/ worthy/young/old/tall/thin/etc.); fear of poverty; fear of ending up like Mom/Grandpa/etc. The list continues. Regardless, the gasoline powering the engine is fear. To compensate for this fear Elvis, Tyson, and Nixon narrowed their vision to one area and ignored everything else, including health.

In many ways, this type of commitment seems laudable and is consistent with some popular thought regarding achievement. Much of the difficulty HAPs experience is with the motivation. By responding to fear, the HAP remains in a state of high anxiety and is perpetually experiencing the fight or flight syndrome. He is in a condition of perpetual stress, probably leading to many medical problems, most of the depression, and probably all overdoses and suicide attempts HAPs experience. It all originates in fear-based motivation. HAPs react to what they're trying to avoid, not what they're attempting to achieve. As a result, they obsess even more intensely. The HAP narrows in on one area and hangs on for dear life. It begins to be the only place she feels comfortable. She latches onto this area like a ship-wrecked sailor gripping a life preserver. As a result, she fails to do the one thing that would save her life—diversify.

Bertrand Russell's quotation states it poetically. To be happy, you must have a wide range of interests. One of the great errors in thought over the past years has been to encourage people to do the opposite. In reality, the human psyche cannot tolerate such obsessiveness. This became increasingly clear to me during my psychotherapy interviews with HAPs. I would ask about their work or careers and actually have to cut them off to continue the session.

Yet I found with more and more frequency their responses to other questions were greeted with blank stares. It was as if I spoke a foreign language. "What are your hobbies?" I'd ask. The result would be either a competitive activity or a curious shrug of the shoulders. "What do you do to relax?" I'd ask. To this question I'd get a brief pause, an uncomfortable clearing of the throat, and the HAP would respond with a question. "Drink?" or "Go to sleep?"

When I asked, "What do you do for fun?" I may as well have asked, "What time does the sun set on Mars?" HAPs have tremendous difficulty even defining fun. Some will actually say sailboat racing or "I compete in ten-kilometer road races." But when you actually observe them, you recognize they're not having fun at all, and it's definitely not relaxing.

Janis Joplin hit like a comet in the night. She had tremendous talent, incredible energy, and she shone brilliantly. Quickly she appeared. Just as dramatically she was gone. Dolly Parton also left a trail of sparks. She's talented, she's energetic, and she sings brilliantly. She has shone for decades and is still quite active. What's the difference? Obviously she is a recording artist and entertainer. Yet she's also an actress, owns a theme park in Pigeon Forge, Tennessee, and writes songs as well as books. Bear Bryant is considered by most people as one of the greatest college football coaches in the history of the sport. He was football for decades. He retired after the 1982 season and died within a year. Tom Landry is considered one of the greatest coaches in the history of professional football. He was the only coach the Dallas Cowboys had in their history until 1986. He stepped down and didn't die. He's involved teaching Sunday school, has other business ventures, and maintains a strong family life.

Mike Tyson lost a heavyweight crown and ended up incarcerated. Evander Holyfield lost the heavyweight crown and now is a speaker at banquets and other meetings. President Nixon was an obsessive-compulsive politician who, according to one biographer, saw it as one of his responsibilities in life to suffer. He did. President Carter was a farmer who saw it as his responsibility to serve. He did and still does. He teaches Sunday school weekly, builds homes for Habitat for Humanity, and negotiates peace settlements around the world. Jimmy Swaggart is an evangelist who preached for years against what he was caught doing. Robert Schuller is a pastor who preaches for people leading healthier lives. He writes books, conducts seminars, and publishes tapes to help people achieve healthier lives. Swaggart resigned from his position in shame. Schuller is still working for healthier living. Whenever you find yourself becoming obsessed with achieving success, you're in trouble. It takes you out of balance and becomes an even greater source of stress. It's important to relax and enjoy even small incremental achievements along the journey of success. Most people put off enjoyment because they haven't achieved "the big one." Yet actually this lack of relaxation can be the very thing that prevents you from achieving.

"I was beginning to wake up a little and realize that the pressures of really getting big and making a lot of money which it looked like was going to happen would destroy the band."
—Stephen Stills of Crosby, Stills and Nash

Diversifying and achieving balance also help avoid a final obstacle to success. After achieving on a big scale, whether you're an athlete, performer, or businessperson, you're faced with a dilemma. Now the stakes are even higher. Michael Jordan became, in the minds of many people, the best basketball player within the history of the sport. At his peak, he retired. Contrary to popular opinion, it was a brilliant decision. He then began playing baseball. People scoffed, but it was even more brilliant. When Jordan came back to basketball, some people attributed his success and enthusiasm to his diversification

High achievement raises the stakes phenomenally and implies new goals that are usually quite unrealistic or impossible to achieve. This is why many people write one book and stop. Or why performers have one hit and then disappear. Or why lottery winners who become overnight millionaires report being far unhappier after the big win than before. It would have been virtually impossible for Michael Jordan to become an even better basketball player. He could only have declined. So instead he diversified. Michael probably wouldn't have returned to basketball if it hadn't been for the baseball players' strike. Since he could do nothing to change that, he attempted to change a controllable situation. He went back to basketball, but he used a different number, forty-five, on his jersey. He also went to a team that did not have a winning record. It was a symbolic statement: "I'm a different player now." In his post-game interview Jordan commented on his relatively low-scoring game: "Now I can only improve. If I'd scored sixty points or more, people would have just said, 'Well, it's Michael,' and how could I improve? Now, I can only get better." So now he has new goals and new direction.

How can Kenny Rogers become an even better singer? He probably can't. So he turned to acting, opened up a restaurant chain, and became involved in several other businesses. Paul Newman? Why did he not experience the Elvis Syndrome? The same reason. He races cars, established a line of gourmet food items, and became involved in benevolent work. People who diversify continue to achieve. People who don't, suffer.

The HAP must find meaning for his or her life beyond the pursuit of success. If achieving becomes the only source of meaning, the HAP will perpetually strive without ever being satisfied. A few lucky people can find meaning in their work. For most, however, work does not provide it. Some find no meaning anywhere in their life. And they face a life of emptiness and pain. Most HAPs think they will find meaning in sheer achievement of success. They are disillusioned when it doesn't turn out that way. As has been mentioned elsewhere in this chapter, it's a mistake to focus externally. This is true because the external things can always disappear. HAPs who seem to adapt the best are those who found at least a portion of their meaning, in activity that is altruistic or in service to others.

Sally Struthers lost her starring role in the long-running TV series *All in the Family*. She has not approached the plateaus of stardom since then. But she is not, on the other hand, self-sabotaging. Her frequent appearances on television now, are for the purpose of helping raise money to feed starving children. She is a prime example of diversification to help maintain the personal sense of balance. Jerry Lewis has done the same thing. When Jerry's comedy stopped, Jerry's Kids began. His efforts have raised enormous amounts of money for others and provided substantial meaning for himself as well. Loretta Swit made us laugh for years in her role as Hot-Lips Houlihan in the TV mega-hit M*A*S*H. Now she joins others who have diversified and finds meaning in altruistic activity. And George Burns doesn't have time to self-destruct. He's got another personal appearance planned. It gives him meaning.

"No vision and you perish; No ideal, and you're lost; Your heart must ever cherish; Some faith at any cost. Some hope, some dream to cling to, Some rainbow in the sky, Some melody to sing to, Some service that is high."
—Harriet Du Autermont

In 1971 I returned home from a year and ten months of combat duty in Vietnam. Like many others of that time I was troubled. At age twenty-two I had personally faced death on both ends of an AK-47 rifle. I was wounded twice, injured in two helicopter crashes, and watched friend and foe die on multiple occasions. By simply picking up a radio handset and making a call, I was able to have anything from jet fighters assisting us to helicopters to take us away. I had been highly decorated for my work in Vietnam and was considering returning there. The natural person to discuss this with was Grandpa. I explained my thoughts to him in detail and it all came down to one dramatic moment.

"So which way you leaning?" he asked after I had explained my thoughts.

"I don't know, Grandpa." I shook my head. "I guess what it comes down to for me is this. I'm twenty-two years old and anything else seems boring. I mean, what do you do for an encore? What can I do that would compare to this? Going back to college would be boring. Football no longer interests me. When you face life and death and all the crap I've gone through over there, nothing else just seems to work for me."

Grandpa paused for a few significant moments. "You can't, Son." He made eye contact with me while leaning over. "You can't do anything like that ever again. Nothing will compare. You can't have an encore so don't try to have one. Don't ever try. You'll never be able to relive the past. Learn from what you did over there. Hell, I'm not ashamed of you. I'm proud of what you've done. We're all proud of you. But now it's time to do something different.

"Go a completely different direction and you can't go wrong. If you try to do some encore performance, the best you can do is relive the past. The worst that can happen is a bullet could get you between the eyes instead of in the leg next time. If you go back over there, you'll never come back. Not that you'll get killed. You'll just be so used to the passion, to the pain, to the adrenaline, that nothing else will ever do. So don't try an encore. Do something different. You'll be better off in the long run. Do something important. Help people. Use what you've learned to help people. That's what you ought to do."

I did what Grandpa said. I didn't agree with him at the time, but I took his advice. Today I believe he was right.

JOURNAL SESSION

1. Discuss whether or not you consider yourself an obsessive-compulsive individual. If you do, describe ways you can turn these characteristics into a positive direction.

2. Describe whether or not you consider your life in balance or out of balance. If you have decided that your life needs to be more balanced, describe ways of doing this.

3. It's difficult for some people to identify superstitions or fears they may have about achieving. If you're able to recognize such beliefs, describe them in detail. If not, give an example from someone else's life or something you've heard or read about indicating it may be "bad luck" to succeed too well.

4. Describe ways you could diversify your own life. Realize the importance of this process and take this assignment seriously. If necessary read over the part of this chapter on diversification.

5. Describe the last time you said yes when you really wanted to say no. Discuss in writing the outcome of that project and how you felt about it. Consider suggesting someone else for the project next time or listing all that you have to do and asking them which of those projects is less important than theirs. Write out a sample reply and rehearse it for the next time you feel cornered and want to say no.

CHECKLIST

Directions: Give yourself a grade on each of the items below. Give yourself an "A" if it describes something you do consistently, "B" for above-average performance, "C" for average, "D" if it's something you rarely do, and "F" if you never do it at all.

____1. I eat at least one hot, balanced meal a day.
____2. I get sufficient sleep to meet my needs.
____3. I give and receive physical and emotional affection.
____4. I have at least one dependable relative within fifty miles.
____5. I exercise to the point of perspiration at least three times per week.
____6. I avoid smoking cigarettes or marijuana.
____7. I avoid consuming alcohol or mind-altering drugs.
____8. I am the appropriate weight for my height.
____9. I have an income adequate to meet basic needs.
____10. I get strength from my religious beliefs.
____11 I regularly attend club or social activities.
____12. I have a network of friends and acquaintances.
____13. I have one or more friends in whom I confide.
____14. I am in good physical health (including eyes, ears, and teeth.)
____15. I am able to speak openly about my feelings.

___16. I have regular calm conversations with family and friends about important daily living issues.

___17. I do something for fun at least once a week.

___18. I am skilled at handling daily minor hassles—traffic, phone, kids, etc.

___19. I avoid consuming caffeine—coffee, tea, or cola drinks.

___20. I take quiet time for myself during the day.

___21. I say no when necessary.

___22. When I'm angry or upset, I talk about it.

___23. I am able to organize my time effectively.

___24. I laugh heartily at least three times per day.

___25. I basically like myself.

___A's ___B's ___ C's ___D's ___F's

How to Score Yourself: For each A give yourself four points, three points for each B, two points for each C, one point for each D, and no points for F's. Add the points up and divide by 25 to find your "Balance Grade-Point Average."

Chapter 9

RETURN TO SENDER
WHEN A GIFT IS NOT A GIFT

"If you achieve success, you will get applause, and if you get applause, you will hear it. My advice to you concerning applause is this: Enjoy it, but never quite believe it."
— *Robert Montgomery, American writer and poet.*

At some point in the evolution of The Elvis Syndrome, our entire office began revolving around it. Writing, speaking, and psychotherapy all involved death by success. Though we have only a small staff, tremendous energy had been generated by the book, seminars, and of course the celebrity of Curtis. Claire, Leah, and LA spent days typing and retyping. Bud pitched a tent in the university library. I wrote, dictated, and traveled to speaking engagements. Curtis had scheduled an appointment in his regular Sunday time block. But on this occasion, Bud and LA asked whether they could sit in for the first few minutes. I had mentioned in a staff meeting that Curtis suggested he wanted to have a brief discussion about Elvis once again. This had been stimulated due to the October 8, 1994 tribute concert in Memphis. I called Curtis and explained Bud's and LA's interest and told him I'd compensate him for his time.

"Lord, yes!" he responded. "You just give me the extra time on the other end. I'll talk about Elvis any day."

I thanked him. "You said you wanted to discuss what could have been done to help Elvis. When I told them, they asked if they could sit in. I know this is a little bit unusual, but they're excited about the book."

"No problem," Curtis explained. "I think Mary will probably want to sit in on it as well. She was going to come with me anyway."

"Great!" I laughed. "We'll make banana splits and have a party," I teased Curtis. Mary had said earlier that Curtis was now addicted to LA's banana splits and had joked ice cream had become his most recent drug of choice.

"You tell LA if she makes banana splits, I'll tell Elvis stories all day long!" Curtis joked. "Mary still doesn't have the combination down quite right."

"We'll work on it!" I laughed.

When Sunday arrived, we moved into the conference room to accommodate the larger-than-normal crowd. We all sat on rocking chairs and had just finished eating the ritual banana splits.

"Are we all Kingophiles yet?" Mary asked, smiling at me.

"Oh, he's coming around." Bud laughed. "He's not a true believer yet. But I am going to get him one of those velvet paintings for Christmas!" We all laughed.

"Did you see that concert?" Curtis asked me.

"I saw parts of it." I nodded. "I fell asleep during the Billy Ray Cyrus segment." Everybody laughed again.

"There was some good music." Curtis smiled. "We drove down there and had some good seats. The pay-per-view probably had a better view than we did. But to me the whole concert demonstrates what an incredible impact Elvis had on music. I mean here we all are, years after his death, still celebrating Elvis Presley. Take a look at the young singers that were there. The fact he's still big enough they'd have tribute today is just phenomenal to me." Curtis made eye contact with me. "I still get real emotional about things like this." He looked up at his wife. "Mary could tell you that." She nodded as Curtis cleared his throat. "I've been goin' over this ever since we first started talkin', way back a year or two ago, whenever it was. It just seems to me like there's something that could have been done to save his life. Since you've been workin' on this idea, have you come up with anything they could have really done? What do you think? Was there anything that could have turned it around for Elvis?"

I shook my head. "Wow! Gee, I really don't know. I think he had gone so far by the end that it was just a matter of *when* he was going to do himself in. Not *if* he was going to. Like everybody else says, I just don't know after his mother's death that he ever really had a life. I mean emotionally. Obviously he experienced tremendous success, but I think maybe when they buried her he really buried his own soul at that point."

"Yeah." Curtis agreed. "He never got over that."

At this point Bud spoke up. "You know, I really believe he would have done whatever the Colonel wanted him to. Everything I have read and everything I remember about those days just tells me Elvis was mesmerized by the Colonel. Maybe that was the big mistake. Either the Colonel got out of touch or the Colonel was just scared if Elvis got help or went into treatment or whatever, it would have been bad for his career. The Colonel was just obsessed with Elvis's career. Maybe not with Elvis, but for God's sake he got fifty percent of everything Elvis made! So it seems to me that his interest was more financial than anything else."

"Maybe so," I responded. "Back then, you've got to remember, treatment wasn't as well accepted as it is now. Especially for stars. Now it's almost unusual if you haven't gotten some kind of treatment and you're a HAP. Things have definitely changed."

Mary gestured toward me. "Well, John. Do you think one of those big family meeting kind of confrontations like we did with Curtis would have worked? If all of them had gotten together and actually confronted Elvis, do you think he would have gotten some help then?"

I paused. The few moments of silence emphasized the question.

"You've had some good results with those, John." LA spoke up. "That one case was a little bit like Elvis's situation. You got everybody in on that one. We didn't even have enough chairs." She laughed.

"Yeah," I nodded. "But—that wasn't Elvis either. And what was that—two and a half years ago? I don't know. Maybe it would have worked. If you could have gotten the Colonel to support it, like Bud said, maybe it would have been successful. The

Colonel, Dr. Nick and anybody else who was prescribing medication, his dad, Priscilla, Ginger, maybe even his daughter if she had been old enough, some of the people from his entourage, yeah."

I sighed. "Maybe that could have worked. I think the Colonel and Priscilla would have been the keys. Even after their divorce, the way I look at it, I think she and the Colonel were the only ones who could have done it. Maybe he would have listened to them. But after his mom's death, I think the only people he really had any respect for were the Colonel and Pricilla."

Curtis leaned forward. "I'm not sure how to say this. How bad—how crazy—was he really? After all the reading and studying you have done on this, how sick or how far gone do you think he really was? I mean, was he psycho or just your garden-variety of alcoholic or what?"

I laughed at Curtis's attempt to be tactful. "Well," I shook my head. "With the drugs and the deification and insulation—I'd say he was in real deep trouble. He could have been pulled out of it. But he was in serious emotional jeopardy and obviously his life was in danger as well. From what I can tell, he was addicted to multiple drugs. He was depressed as he could possibly be. He was out of touch with reality. He was terminally lonely. At the end—maybe without a true friend in his life—although there were a lot of people who loved him—his entire entourage worshiped him. But to me, that's not a friend. He was in a mess. But I think he could have been pulled out of it with the right help. I'll put it this way. I have seen a lot worse situations get better."

Bud quit rocking, leaned over, placed his elbows on his knees, and looked at me. "So what do you think would have made the difference? If you had been there on the scene, say a week or two before his death. There you were in August, July, June, whatever, 1977. You're his shrink. What would you have done if you'd had the authority?"

I sighed deeply and leaned back in my rocking chair. "Goodness, gracious," I rubbed my forehead with my right hand. "You know," I coughed. "It's real easy for me to sit here and do the big-expert-after-the-fact routine. I'm pretty objective now. You know, I wasn't there! If I had been, there's a chance I could have been as caught up in all the fame and glory and insanity as everybody else. You know, I'd like to think not! Especially if my job was to be his personal lifeguard. Maybe I could have been more objective. But from this angle—what are we, seventeen years later looking back on it?—I'd say there's a wide variety of things that could have been done. It's like one of the first times we talked about this, Curtis. You said he needed a lifeguard instead of a bodyguard." I gestured toward Curtis. "Well, he sure as the world did! But he's not the only one. And there was a time in your life, Curtis, when you could have used one. Bud, there have been several times in your life when you could have used a lifeguard!" Everybody laughed along with Bud.

"I believe that his entourage did almost everything wrong that could have possibly been done. And so did Elvis. If they could have changed just one of several things, it might have turned it all around. But to answer in the context in which the question was asked, it all comes down to him—the one individual who could have made that decision—Elvis. He would have to go along with it. I mean, we could have knocked him out and taken him to Minnesota, Sierra Tucson, Betty Ford, or anywhere. But they couldn't make him get better. The HAP has to want to get healthy—he has to want to give up the drugs—or whatever it is that is taking him to the edge. I obviously don't know that it was ever there with Elvis."

I turned toward Mary. "I probably would have tried to orchestrate some sort of intervention, that kind of family confrontation you were referring to. I would have probably tried to do that. And I've seen a lot of those work. In fact, if they're done right, I've never seen one fail. But it's like I said before, we'd have to have a lot of cooperation, and from what I can tell most people, except for Priscilla and the Colonel, were intimidated by him. They worshiped him, they adored him, they idolized him. But they were scared of him. He was their employer—as well as being Elvis Presley. And you know that's one thing that most people can't understand. He was *so big!*"

"There is really is nobody to compare him with today, is there?" Mary asked.

"No!" I spoke immediately. "No, not even close. Younger folks can't really appreciate and understand the impact Elvis Presley had. There was just simply nobody you could compare him to. Nobody close. He's bigger than Schwarzenegger, Michael Jackson, and Garth Brooks all put together. But there's one thing I'm sure of. The bigger they are, the more lifeguards they probably need. Not to protect them from others but to save them from themselves. This death by success is real! And you don't have to be some celebrity to get it. Curtis, you told me the driver of the tour bus for your group got picked up for drunken driving and lost his job. What was he making? Thirty thousand a year? Now he's working in the carpet mills making one-third the amount he used to. Anybody and everybody can get it. This whole thing is bigger than we ever imagined when we first started talking about it."

"Only friends will tell you the truths you need to hear to make the last part of your life bearable."
—Francine DuPlessix Gray

Regardless of notoriety or potential of the HAP, at some point the pattern must be interrupted. There are two different approaches that can be taken to accomplish this. One strategy is preventive, and the other we will call therapeutic. Therapeutic strategies will be discussed further in Chapter Ten. Prevention has been discussed earlier, and will be synthesized in this chapter. Approaching the HAP at the foundation level will create change regardless of how far advanced he or she may be. Most of these foundations have been discussed elsewhere in this book. These are summarized, and brought together in this chapter to give you more of an idea on how to create change.

The first place to start is with the family. Family is critical in the early developmental stages of the Elvis Syndrome. It can be equally critical in healing the pain. This is true whether you are focusing on marriage or extended family. HAPs are usually quite sensitive people, though at times it may be masked. It is common for a HAP to have his or her defense mechanisms up most of the time. But they will lower them around family. So they may appear unaffected by a scathing professional review, but crushed by a much less significant gesture from a family member.

Cow Pies experienced this in an earlier marriage. He had been working on a very difficult creative project, and faced several obstacles. Finally, he laid the project out on a story board in his home office and achieved a missing breakthrough. Filled with excitement and near-jubilance, he described it as the closest thing to a "eureka" enlightenment he'd ever experienced. Anxious to share it with anyone, Cow Pies asked his wife and oldest son to listen and then began to explain excitedly what he had discovered.

"She sat there with her damn arms crossed with this real bored, apathetic look on her face," he explained. "After I got through talking about it she didn't say a word. She just turned and walked out of the room! She acted like I'd interrupted her or something. I really didn't expect her to understand. But she could have at least appreciated it. I was *so* let down. My son was more pumped about it than she. And he had no idea what I was talking about . . . ."

F. Scott Fitzgerald, Ernest Hemingway, Elvis Presley, and countless other HAPs had tremendous difficulty with marriages. It is probably the most critical relationship a HAP ever experiences. Their complex personality nature makes them difficult mates. Idealistic and romantic, they sometimes lean toward infatuation or even unfaithfulness. However, such trysts are usually only temporary and occur after such interactions as described above with Cow Pies'. The HAP's introverted, creative nature makes him or her highly vulnerable to the few with whom he's truly honest. HAPs have very few friends. The spouse is usually the closest, until the sensitivities have been damaged. At this point the HAP will begin to withdraw. Incidentally, in Cow Pies' case, his son is still around. But the wife is gone!

HAPs with strong marriages seem to have an advantage in avoiding the Elvis Syndrome. Charlton Heston, Paul Newman, and Vice President Al Gore are each examples. President Carter, Billy Crystal, and Garth Brooks are HAPs who have built healthy marriages, although there may have been struggles. This foundation, along with a strong extended family, is likely the most powerful place to intervene. If you are a HAP, get into marriage counseling immediately, at least for a diagnostic check. If you're married to a HAP, do your best to entice him or her into counseling.

Strong extended family relationships are also important. This may be the reason Michael Jackson is able to survive the accusations he experienced without resorting to suicide. The fact his family aggressively and openly supported him at an extremely unpopular moment could have been his figurative salvation. Barbara Mandrell is another example of a HAP with incredibly strong family ties. Her father, Irby, was her manager, and for years accompanied her on tour. Her sisters were also part of her backup vocal group.

If you don't have a strong family relationship, try to get help and reconcile it. If you can't, build a new family around you. Either way, the importance of the family network cannot be overlooked. If you decide to build a new family around you, be very selective and purposeful. Actually enlist someone to be a father or mother figure. Choose new siblings. Don't leave it up to genetics or biology this time. Choose it yourself. A strong marriage and family provides roots, stability, and helps maintain balance. It will help you survive the multiple challenges of the Elvis Syndrome.

"Successful men usually snatch success from seeming failure. If they know that there is such a word as defeat, they will not admit it. They may be whipped, but they are not aware of it."
—Thomas Jefferson

Other foundations are important as well. Probably the second-most significant foundation is a strong friendship network. True friends can help the HAP avoid death by success or interrupt the journey if he is already in the advanced stages. In some cases the friendship network is more powerful than family, especially if the family is fragmented or distant. Regardless, the same principles apply to both groups. In many ways the friendship network can play a positive role in helping avoid deification. The mere presence of friends can create an anchor. Several years ago I met a

HAP who had grown very wealthy in real estate development. After a few discussions, he said he realized who I was. "Good Lord!" he laughed aloud. "You're Loisey's son. Why if it hadn't been for her, I'd never made it through high school. I used to copy off her tests. She even did my homework for me. That woman's a genius!" It's not hard to be humble, even if you're a millionaire when you're reminded of your origins. Friends provide that reminder and act as an anchor.

A story told about Elvis illustrates HAPs actually want those friends. He was standing outside a theater in Memphis when a car with two of his former high school classmates drove by. The car slowed, as the passengers looked out. When they saw it was Elvis, they sped away. Elvis reportedly turned to his companion and lamented, "A few years ago they would have stopped and talked to me." It's difficult for a HAP to actually trust the people whom he grows close to after his success. He fears they only want to be close to him because of his money or success, not because of who he is. The friends he had prior to notoriety most often are unsure of how to relate and most often shy away. Yet these would be the friends actually most helpful to the HAP. Dolly Parton's childhood friend who accompanies her is a prime example of how this can help. This person is Dolly's traveling companion and assistant, who is with her constantly when she is on the road. Dolly has described her as being an anchor to an otherwise hectic lifestyle. Usually, employees don't serve that function well. Because the HAP has power to financially affect the person, the feedback and input could be artificially altered. A friend is someone who will look you in the eye, shake you to get your attention, and hold the mirror of reality up to your face. Everybody needs one.

Many years ago the late Dr. Karl Menninger was asked what was the most helpful piece of advice he would offer a depressed person. Apparently, after thinking about the question, Dr. Menninger suggested: "I'd tell them to find someone more depressed than they are and help that person." That's astounding when you realize Dr. Menninger was probably the most renowned and prolific psychiatrist this country has ever produced. He didn't recommend medication or hospitalization.

Instead, he thought it more important for the depressed person to focus away from himself.

It's a profound comment and introduces the next foundation. It is becoming involved in a cause greater than yourself that provides meaning. That cause can be any of a number of things, but it helps you focus elsewhere. Most HAPs are deeply spiritual people, though not necessarily in the traditional sense. Some can easily find such meaning within formal religion. Others find it elsewhere. The examples are endless. Hundreds of comedians have participated in an immensely successful fund raiser, *Comic Relief*, led by Billy Crystal, Robin Williams, and Whoopi Goldberg. Literally thousands of homeless people have benefited. Musicians pitched in for the "We Are The World " campaign led by Quincy Jones and Bob Geldoff to raise funds for starving children in Africa. Recently, Garth Brooks, James Taylor, Stevie Wonder and others gave a fund-raising concert on cable television. Having a cause greater than yourself is very important. If you don't have one, it is not difficult to find. If you're involved with a HAP, this is one of the easiest places to intervene. It will help the HAP become less narcissistic and have less difficulty with deification.

The final foundation in this section is one that is sensitive and probably most critical. Yet is also one of the most difficult places to intervene. An entire chapter has been devoted to alcohol and drugs. I strongly suggest you read it again! The foundation is one of moderation and sobriety. Since most HAPs have tremendous denial about this problem, it is almost impossible to get their attention. If you know a HAP who doesn't have an alcohol or drug problem, you're both in luck!

Since most HAPs are highly obsessive-compulsive, addiction rates run high among this group. A simple rule I have found can work. Most scientific researchers today agree. One to two ounces of alcohol every twenty-four hours probably is not unhealthy and may even be constructive. At the same time, scientists have discovered more than two ounces every twenty-four hours leads to soaring rates of diminishing returns. If a HAP can limit alcohol consumption to that level—two beers, two six-ounce glasses of wine, or one standard-size mixed drink—there is no scientific reason to abstain. Most can't. In that case, I suggest abstinence. Chapter Ten gives an example of one way to confront a HAP who refuses help. I attempt to leave all emotions out of the picture when discussing alcohol use. Anything more than two ounces of alcohol every twenty-four hours is unhealthy. Let science be your guide.

> *"When one door closes, another opens.*
> *But we often look so long and so regretfully upon the closed door*
> *that we do not see the one which was opened for us."*
> —*Alexander Graham Bell*

There are four additional foundations to overcoming or avoiding the Elvis Syndrome. The first of these was discussed in Chapter Eight. Diversity is one of the major qualities in maintaining balance. It is also probably the primary avenue for preventing the Elvis Syndrome. By diversifying, the HAP's foundation is wider and stronger. Dolly Parton, Kenny Rogers, and former President Jimmy Carter were all mentioned as good examples of diversification.

In one case I made a recommendation for diversification that had unexpectedly good results. I suggested to a HAP she begin attending Toastmasters as a way of improving her communication skills. She complied after some hesitation, and finally found a club where she felt comfortable. She not only improved her communication skills, but began winning speaking contests. She met someone through one of the speaking competitions who directed her toward a new career. Her income tripled in thirteen months. That's a bit more than diversification, and the results were fascinating. It seems to prove the point that a HAP will turn anything into a contest.

Eric Fromm, the great philosopher and psychotherapist, said, "The deepest need of man then, is the need to overcome his separateness, to leave the prison of his aloneness. The absolute failure to do this means insanity." Fromm's comments speak to the power of insulation and isolation. This is one of the biggest problems HAPs face. It's a seductive trap, considering their introverted nature. HAPs who deal with people regularly as part of their responsibilities need time to recuperate. The problem is, with increased isolation, the HAP loses further contact with reality. This allows deification to not only occur, but grow. As indicated in earlier chapters, the feedback available to Romans through their tradition needs to be accessible today. On many occasions, HAPs don't want to hear feedback, but it's definitely what they need. By diversifying sometimes the feedback is provided automatically.

An additional foundation is the ability to face suffering and struggle. Many attempt to avoid suffering by drug or alcohol use. That course usually makes the problem worse. Others use pure psychological denial, thereby increasing suffering in the long term. Occasionally, it appears things have come so easily to the HAP, that he or she simply never learned to struggle. She responds as though if struggle is necessary something must be wrong. If it comes easily, it was meant to be. Learning to welcome suffering and face adversity is vital to overcoming the Elvis Syndrome. It also adds depth to the personality of a HAP, which helps avoid death by success altogether.

I've encouraged many advanced-level HAPs to attend Outward Bound and National Outdoor Leadership Schools (NOLS). These outdoor adventure-based programs are far better in many cases than psychiatric hospitalization. If a HAP is in the advanced stages of alcoholism or drug dependency, I recommend Outward Bound or NOLS only after he or she has gone through a medically-supervised detoxification program. The reason I prefer such programs is their individual emphasis on facing and overcoming adversity. I truly believe certain HAPs have gone through not only life-changing but life-saving experiences as well during their times at Outward Bound or NOLS. I have recommended these programs both preventively and therapeutically dozens of times. I have faced many HAPs who didn't want to go at first, but I have never had one who didn't complete the course. I've heard only one negative complaint. That was from a lady who accurately claims she didn't get to shower enough. The process you go through in these programs revolves around facing adversity and struggling on an intensely personal level. Yet they allow you to succeed. It is a drug-free and work-schedule-free environment. I give both of these schools my highest recommendations.

There are two final characteristic foundations. The first is being able to channel your obsessive-compulsive energy in a healthy direction. This was discussed in detail elsewhere in this book. In summary, I suggest you avoid fighting obsessive-compulsive energy. You can't win. Rather, obsess about being healthy. Be compulsively balanced. If you're able to do this, you will be happier and healthier than you could ever dream possible. Take a hint from the lady mentioned in Chapter Five. Schedule a healthy lifestyle regimen and then follow it compulsively.

The final foundation is developing the necessary emotional equipment to deal with your life. This is an ongoing process, not something you do once and then stop. It can be accomplished predominantly on your own. There are literally dozens of audio and videocassette learning programs to help you in this area. You can get hours of inexpensive psychotherapy in your car while commuting. Seminars and weekend workshops are plentiful and relatively inexpensive. You can also find excellent books on subjects ranging from self-esteem, to happiness, to dealing with specific kinds of problems. All of these are available at little cost.

I do recommend HAPs get physical exams annually, regardless of age. I also suggest annual consultations with a professional psychotherapist who specializes in helping high performers. These appointments are preventive in nature and that needs to be clarified at the time the appointment is made. Many organizations provide consultants exclusively for this purpose. These visits are very non-threatening and are actually enjoyable. Just as a medical exam can detect problems before they become unmanageable, so can a good psychotherapist. I've seen such visits actually prevent disaster, and occasionally—just in time. This can help you maintain a sense of balance, draw healthy boundaries and also assist in saying "return to sender."

"The man who masters himself is delivered from
the force that binds all creatures."
—Goethe

When I was a judo student in Japan, I was told a story about a senior monk who was meditating when a student attempted to interrupt him. Try as he might, the student could not detract the monk from his meditative state. After a long time had passed and in spite of continued aggravation from the student, the senior monk rose from his meditation.

"Master," the student implored. "How were you able to maintain your focus and concentration while I was bothering you?"

After pausing a moment, the monk responded, "When someone offers you a gift, it's not yours unless you accept it."

There are times in your life when gifts will be offered that you need not accept. There will be other occasions when you want to accept a gift but after close inspection you realize it's not a gift at all. When a well-intentioned person offers you alcohol or drugs, as an example, it's usually not a gift. The giver could have fully intended it to be a gift, but as the Spartans discovered, sometimes a gift horse is filled with surprises. Cow Pies was offered a healthy sum of money to sleep with a stranger's wife for her birthday! He met the man for the first time in a bar. Within minutes, this man offered him five hundred dollars to go home with him, crawl into his wife's bed and pretend he was the husband. Then, he was supposed to wake up the man's wife and have sex with her. "She loves you," the stranger explained. "She thinks you're wonderful!" Thankfully, Cow Pies didn't accept the proposition. It was not a gift for him or the man's wife.

I've heard similar stories from a variety of HAPs. This is not an uncommon occurrence for athletes, entertainers, or other high-achievers. Stephen King's novel, entitled *Misery*, took this process to a frightening yet entertaining conclusion. In the book, King's main character is an author who has an automobile accident and is kidnapped and held captive by an obsessive fan. James Caan starred in a movie adaptation of King's book. *Saturday Night Live* did a skit with Dana Carvey playing the role of the Church Lady revolving around King's novel. Caan's costar from the movie played opposite the Church Lady in the skit. Both the book and the movie investigated a fan's obsession with a HAP.

HAPs have told me of being offered any imaginable gift. Several have been offered cars. Sex is a fairly common gift. One singer was offered an ostrich. It was actually shipped to her home. Most have been offered the use of vacation homes and accommodations. An attorney I worked with was offered the proceeds from over a hundred acres of marijuana—not as payment but simply as a gift.

This is one of the times when personal boundaries are vitally important. Your identity and values must be very clear and certain, both to you and ultimately to others. You can say no in a respectful manner without alienating anyone or appearing to be rude. This is usually something HAPs must practice and perhaps even memorize.

Most people mean well. It makes them feel important to offer a gift. By giving to a high performer, they are coming close to touching or sharing in his fame or glory. Actually, most people who offer gifts do it indirectly for themselves. They often feel better for having given than the HAP does for receiving. Their gestures are not necessarily altruistic, but their intentions are— usually at least—harmless.

The stranger who offered Cow Pies a night with his wife was sincere. Certainly the stranger himself would have received no benefit. Cow Pies was relatively sure it wasn't some twisted version of a sex game the stranger had in mind. The stranger even pulled out a picture of his wife to prove she was relatively attractive!

"I was overwhelmed," he explained to me. "At first I was shocked. I thought it was a practical joke. Then I got really pissed off when I realized this was serious. I thought he was some kind of a weirdo or something. Then I just went back into shock again. Two or three days later, I guess I thought it was a little bit funny. But at the time I didn't think it was funny at all.

"He was drunk. And I was about half drunk myself. If I'd been any drunker, I would probably have agreed to it. I damn sure needed the money. But somebody could have gotten shot or stabbed or something. His wife could have shot both of us! When he sobered up, he could have shot me! It could have been a real bad scene."

Sometimes a gift is not a gift. It's definitely not yours unless you accept it. On most occasions it is best to simply "return to sender."

"We have no more right to consume happiness without producing it than to consume wealth without producing it."
—George Bernard Shaw

In October 1994, I conducted a series of seminars in northern Ontario, Canada. I was speaking on the topic of self-destructiveness and suicide. As part of my tour, I was interviewed at several radio stations. The announcer's questions focused on John Candy. He had met John on several occasions and considered him borderline suicidal. One announcer described John as a family-oriented man and a good parent but one who was prone to excess. "He smoked too much, ate too much obviously, and, for a period of his life, drank and took drugs too much."

He asked me if I thought Candy had Elvised out. We had discussed it in detail. I made the general comment that I thought all successful entertainers—especially comedians—had trouble with self-sabotage. The next caller asked me to continue that discussion.

"What about Pee-Wee Herman? Why didn't he commit suicide?" the caller asked.

"He did," I responded.

There was brief pause. "No, he didn't," the caller disagreed. "He's still around. He was in *Buffy, the Vampire Slayer* and he was also in one of the *Batman* movies. You ought to check your facts."

"Well, I guess you and I disagree." I smiled. "Now, I think Pee-Wee Herman's dead. Paul Reubens, that's who you're talking about. He's still alive. And apparently he's doing quite well, all things considered. But Pee-Wee Herman—he's dead and gone in my opinion. I think he's buried, though I'm not sure where. Probably somewhere in Sarasota."

"Oh, I get it." The caller laughed. "You're saying they're two different people. What is it? Like schizophrenia or something, ay? Like *Sibyl* or the *Three Faces of Eve* or one of those kind of things? You're saying Paul Reubens is alive and Pee-Wee

Herman is dead. In fact, they are the same person. Maybe they're two personalities but they're the same person. Is that it?"

I shifted my body close to the microphone and shook my head. "I don't know. I honestly have never met either Pee-Wee or Paul Reubens, frankly. So I can't speak with absolute authority. But I've got my opinion about this. I think Paul Reubens is probably a fine actor who through chance, or destiny, or genius, created Pee-Wee Herman. And then Pee-Wee Herman kind of took control of Paul. I guess in some ways it's like a body giving birth to cancer and then the cancer destroys the body. I think this is pretty much what happened. I think that Pee-Wee took over Paul Reubens' life. And frankly, I don't think Paul liked it. I'm sure he liked the money and all that. But, in the end, I think Paul Reubens hated Pee-Wee.

"I know the last year his show was supposed to be on, Paul had worked extremely hard to get two years worth of tapes in the can so he could take a break. I think he was burned out with the role, but the role was so powerful that he couldn't just leave it behind. You know it's like Paul Reubens was still an unknown, but Pee-Wee on the other hand—he was succeeding. I mean, Pee-Wee was an incredible success.

"When was Paul Reubens arrested? Sometime in 1991? Whenever it was, he told the detectives, 'I'm Pee-Wee Herman.' I think he was right. I think it was Pee-Wee Herman who did that. It was Pee-Wee who self-destructed. He's the one who 'Elvised out.' But still—I think Paul's okay. I don't mean to seem melodramatic. But it could have been that Pee-Wee had to die for Paul to be able to live."

"Oh, wow!" the caller answered. "This is getting deep. You're telling me that Pee-Wee Herman went through death by success or whatever you call it. And by doing so, Paul Reubens is ready to go on. But Paul Reubens isn't successful like Pee-Wee was."

"Well, yeah, that may be true." I nodded. "But one of the things I've learned over the past several years is that success without happiness is not all that it might appear to be from the outside looking in. We may think having the cars, money, and all that goes along with success is a big deal. But if you don't have the happiness to take with you, you're still going to be miserable.

"Paul Reubens was miserable being Pee-Wee Herman. He may be far wealthier with Pee-Wee, but my belief is he probably made the right decision. 'Kill that idiot off and let me be myself!' That doesn't mean the mechanism he used, for goodness sake, to kill Pee-Wee was healthy or the right way. Dana Carvey quit doing the Church Lady and maybe for the same reason. I mean, the Church Lady was going to take over his life. And maybe he didn't want her to. Maybe he wasn't going to be happy with that. So I think Dana did the right thing and I think Paul did the right thing. I admire him for putting Pee-Wee away. I'm sorry about the way it happened. But he probably did the right thing."

I have replayed that conversation in my mind several times since then and have put tremendous thought into it. Right or wrong, I don't know. I don't even know that Paul Reubens could explain what he did and why he did it. However, I do believe Paul decided Pee-Wee Herman was not a gift. I think he made the right decision when he decided Pee-Wee was to be "returned to sender."

JOURNAL SESSION

1. Describe your friends who would risk confronting you if you were involved in self-destructive behavior. If you can think of someone, it might be important to identify these people in writing and give them permission to confront you should the occasion arise.

2. Describe a time where someone may have confronted you on something you were doing that was unhealthy or self-destructive. It may have been a teacher when you were a child. It may have been someone as an adult. Describe the process in detail and your reaction to it.

3. Describe your strongest and weakest foundations for avoiding the Elvis Syndrome. Analyze each and discuss what steps you can take to strengthen those that are weak.

4. Think of a time when someone offered you a gift that you recognized—then or later—was not really a gift. Discuss your
   reaction to the gift and to the giver.

5. Discuss in writing whether you still possess gifts that need to
   be "returned to sender." Choose one and discuss how to "give
   it back." Discuss whether a ritual of some kind might not help
   you do this. Give some thought to designing a going-away ritual to say "goodbye." Review the chapter for ideas.

CHECKLIST

Directions: Check those that apply to you.

___1. One or both of my parents has died. I did not attend a
   funeral for at least one.
___2. Sometimes it seems that I can carry my parents around
   inside my head. I can hear exactly what they would say
   to me in certain situations.
___3. I have a brother or sister who died. I wasn't able to
   attend the funeral because of financial or job considerations.
___4. I don't have any friends who know me well enough to
   intervene if or when I become self-destructive.
___5. I don't have any family members who would be able to
   intervene if I needed help. They either live too far away
   to know what's going on, or I don't have that kind of relationship with them.
___6. I know there are incidents in my life that need to be dealt
   with, but I've been ignoring them because I don't have
   time.
___7. I am not a member of a church or service organization.
___8. Others have told me on more than one occasion that I
   need to get counseling.
___9. I have few ties to my hometown and few friends who've
   known me longer than five years.
___10. Those closest to me are employees of mine or part of my
   entourage. Few would be considered peers.

How to Score Yourself: Total the check marks. More than five checks suggests a lack of foundations necessary to prevent the Elvis Syndrome. Use the Journal Session to help determine where to strengthen your foundations to avoid problems. Consider numbers four and five carefully and take action to give written permission to several people to act as your lifeguards.

Chapter 10

Getting Off of Lonely Street
OVERCOMING THE ELVIS SYNDROME

"This is the greatest sin of you and me and all of us. To have more power than love; more knowledge than understanding; more information about the earth than the people who live in it; more skill to fly to far off places than to stop a moment and look within our own heart."
—Lillian Smith

Paul Reubens was featured in *Batman 2* as the Penguin's father. In the movie he throws the young penguin over a bridge, into the water. The penguin floats away in a small baby basket and is only heard from many years later, in Danny DeVito drag.

I have another fantasy. Paul places his Pee-Wee Herman paraphernalia within the same basket and *it* floats down the same river. Paul waves goodbye as the hair grease, bow tie, and high-water plaid trousers fade toward the setting sun. Pee-Wee is a gift Paul had accepted. But now it was time to say goodbye—not in the falsetto character voice but in the mature and solemn farewell. Paul whisks away a tear because there was both good and bad in the character. He acknowledges the good, but it was time to say goodbye.

A gift can be an attribute, behavior, or trait. There are many gifts you don't need to accept at all. There are others you accept at one time in your life and later give away or discard. There are some gifts you may accept at one point and not only decide, but find it vital, to return later. It's relatively common, as an example, for a five-year-old to have a tantrum because he wants a toy. Yet for a thirty-five-year-old to have a similar tantrum is at the best weird. It's not unusual for an eight-year-old whose team loses the ball game to cry. However, when a fifty-eight-year-old does the same thing, there is a bit of a problem. Anger may help you survive an abusive childhood. The same anger, if taken into your marriage many years later, can destroy it. Similarly, fear or anger may be appropriate in one marriage. The same response can and often does destroy your second marriage.

Some problems with death by success simply can be avoided or managed. The impulse arises and you can decide not to react. Other problems can be overcome by focusing on the foundation level as discussed in Chapter Nine. As we indicated earlier, if it's an unhealthy family network, your family can be rebuilt. You can attempt to reconcile the relationship. If that isn't possible, you can choose another relationship. If your role model is insufficient you can easily find others through biographies, tapes, and mentor relationships. If low self-esteem or guilt is a problem, you can enter psychotherapy, attend seminars, or read one of the many fine books on the subject. Those people who have insufficient outlets for creativity can find adequate outlets. There are a many ways to avoid or manage some forms of self sabotage. Others, however, are more difficult.

Negative programming and other problems often result from multiple years of socialization and learning. Many times, the learning has come from parental role models or other authority figures and consequently is extremely difficult to overcome. Other times, the learning has resulted from trauma that unconsciously or consciously left its mark. The St. Louis talk-show brother mentioned earlier is a good example. He was responding to dramatic negative programming yet totally unaware of it: *It is okay to be mediocre, but don't be too successful. If you are, something terrible will happen.* His entire adult life he lived by this theme. When he came to the point that relative success was within grasp, he would drink to insure self-sabotage and return to mediocrity. Like Paul Reubens, he needed to say goodbye to some gifts. Once he did, happiness and success awaited him. But it did not occur easily. He worked vigorously to overcome these patterns and followed most of the principles described in this chapter.

I read many years ago accounts of Ivan Pavlov's early studies with dogs that led to much of early psychological thought regarding conditioning. The first accounts I read indicated it took Pavlov approximately twenty-eight consecutive days to condition the dogs successfully. Later accounts say that it was twenty-one days. Either way the point is the same. If you want to change a deep-rooted self-sabotage habit it will take more than simply skimming over this chapter. Nor will the typical Type A obsessive-compulsive approach succeed. Devoting twenty-eight minutes instead of twenty-eight days to overcoming the problem will result in frustration at one extreme and increased cynicism at the other.

It will take serious effort to change the habits. The journal assignments and suggestions listed after each chapter up to this point provide you an opportunity to begin such work. If they are incomplete at this point, you can benefit greatly by beginning them. You may need to discuss your completed work with a friend or a counselor to help you achieve more clarity. The goal is to grow more aware. At some point, however, you have to go beyond consciousness. Awareness alone is rarely enough. You will need to say goodbye.

"You can do very little with faith, but you can do nothing without it."
—Samuel Butler

Closure is important. Our minds seek closure like a guided missile or a smart-bomb seeks its destination. Just as the bomb will go around trees or underneath a bridge, so does the mind aim for completeness. It does it in small ways that may seem insignificant. When it comes to intense issues, lack of closure can destroy your life.

For example, perhaps you have sung along with a tune on the car radio but, when you reach your destination, turn it off before it's done. Hours later, the song comes back to your mind for no apparent reason. You begin thinking about it. Several more hours and you're humming it once again. And later that evening, as you prepare for bed, you're whistling the same tune out loud. It's unfinished and incomplete. This is what some people call the repetition compulsion. There are two ways to remember this. *That which you fail to complete, repeats.* Virtually anything you don't get closure on will resurface in your mind or life. If you don't complete the tune from the example above, it will intrude into your thoughts continuously. You will claim it's outside your control and explain, "It just comes to me." Certainly, it appears to just come to you. What you don't understand is, it comes to you because you are hanging on to it. You are not finishing it. Complete it, and then there is closure.

Another way to remember the importance of this process is: *That which you repress, expresses.* This may seem like a paradox, but it means exactly what it says. If you try to force the tune out of your mind, it will express itself in one way or another. To say "I'm just going to forget it" is then to be awakened from a deep sleep unable to clear your mind of the song. To say, "I'm not going to think about it" is to inevitably face the problem even more intensely or aggressively than ever imagined.

It's all "unfinished business." To finish business you sit down, hum the tune through to its conclusion and then go back to sleep. That's rather simple but it's exactly what you must do to get closure. There are other tunes in your life that aren't as easy to complete. But they're even more necessary. The basis for most avenues leading to the Elvis Syndrome is unfinished business. After studying the death and life of Elvis Presley, I sincerely believe that if he had gotten closure on his own unfinished business, he would probably be alive today. He indeed may have gone through a bankruptcy or two. He definitely needed to be treated for multiple drug addictions. But most of all, I sincerely believe he died how and when he did because he didn't finish business surrounding his mother's death. I believe he grieved himself to death after her loss. He probably relived the death so redundantly it became the center of his focus. He played the tune over and over again in his mind. Before long he had the entire tune memorized. In the end it wasn't coincidence. He had the tune memorized and he played it out in his own life. And in his death.

In the same way I'm convinced I would be dead today were it not for finishing the same kind of business. So might the St.

Louis talk-show brother. And the Sin Eater. And MDWIFE. And Cow Pies. And Topanga Canyon. And Curtis. And many others.

Yet maybe it's not a life-or-death matter with your unfinished business. Perhaps it's just pain, or misery, or loneliness. Guess what? You don't have to live with those tunes either. It's time you finished business.

"There are two things to aim at in life: first to get what you want; and, after that, to enjoy it. Only the wisest of men can achieve the second."
—Logan Pearsall Smith

I originally met Curtis after his Tucumcari episode. It was an inglorious introduction from his perspective. Though I didn't know it at the time, it was indirectly the beginning of this book. His wife, Mary, contacted me when Curtis called her from Tucumcari. She'd gotten my name from a book I had written five years earlier. Our goal, frankly, became to force him into treatment for alcoholism. Yet, in a deeper sense, I came to realize we were all forcing him to face the unfinished business in his life. It was time for Curtis to complete his tune.

There are many times you must force people to get help. This concept seems foreign to many. I see it as quite logical. If you had a family member or friend who needed emergency medical treatment and didn't want to get it, you would simply force him to. If the person said, "No, I don't want to get my broken leg treated. Just ignore the bone sticking out of my skin there. I don't want to get help," you would ultimately ignore his protest and get emergency help. Most of us would do the same. However, most believe alcoholism, drug addiction, or other emotional problems should be dealt with differently. In reality the only difference is in your perception.

Mary perceived correctly that Curtis was facing an emergency. She and I have re-created our original meeting with Curtis. For this book, we changed a few circumstances to protect identities of those involved. You are encouraged to follow Mary's example if you attempt confronting a friend or family member. It is best, in all cases, to use a counselor or clergyperson trained in

this type of intervention. Such meetings can have absolutely disastrous results. Or they can be the beginning of health. The difference is usually found in two factors: the skill level of the professional person involved and the commitment and sincerity of
those in attendance.

We practiced the meeting with Curtis three times to let the
participants know what to expect and to measure their commitment. These meetings are stressful and incredibly painful for all
involved. It was very important for everyone to have a clear idea
of the procedure, possible outcomes, and pressures. The list of
participants included Mary; their two daughters, Lacey, age
twenty, and Shannon, age seventeen; Curtis's manager, Ike;
Curtis's mother, Miriam; his minister, Bob; his lead guitarist,
Flip; his sister, Margaret, and brother-in-law, Fred; and his
friend and fellow singer, J.T. I directed each of them to be calm
and unemotional in our meeting with Curtis. Each person also
brought personal letters I had reviewed at an earlier meeting.
The letters were very objective and rational summaries of things
they had noticed indicating Curtis suffered a severe alcohol problem. I suspected it might not take a great deal of convincing.
From all I had heard, after his Tucumcari experience, Curtis was
already frightened, but we weren't taking any chances.

The group convened for the intervention at Bob's church.
Curtis was a member there but hadn't attended in years. He had
met several times with Bob, who had served as a friend and con-
fidante. J.T. had been in the country music business even longer
than Curtis and was considered one of the true old-timers in
Nashville. He had actually warned Curtis on several occasions of
following in Elvis's footsteps a little too closely. At the time,
Curtis really had not understood. Ike had done the same. He had
known Curtis's father extremely well and in fact had worked at
WSM Radio with his father forty years earlier. He had watched
Curtis grow up and was in many ways his father figure as well as
manager. I considered these three men to be the emotional back-
bone of our intervention.

When Curtis walked in I was almost jolted. He looked thin
and pale with dark, hollow eyes. Mary led him in and seemed to
be almost holding him up by his left arm. He appeared older than

Ike, though I knew he was probably twenty-five years younger.

"Curtis," I gestured toward one of the empty chairs in the circle. "I'm John Baucom. I'm here with your friends. Have a seat."

Curtis stopped and began glancing around the group cautiously. He looked so confused I thought he might have been heavily medicated. Mary had assured me that it wasn't the case.

"Curtis," I spoke up again. "I know this may be a bit confusing. These people are here to talk to you. They all love you a whole lot. They've asked me to sort of organize and moderate this meeting, but it's their idea. They want to talk to you about some stuff, and we're going to ask you to just listen. After they're done, you'll have a chance to respond. Do you have any questions for me right now?" Curtis looked over at me and shook his head.

"No," he frowned. "I don't know what this is all about. I don't know who you are. But I guess the main thing is, can I smoke?" Several people laughed nervously and Bob responded.

"Now, Curtis, you've been a member here for twenty years. You know we don't let people smoke in the church!" Curtis smiled and cleared his throat.

"This really won't take that long." I assured him. "Each person is going to read you a brief letter. The letters are to you. Again, I'm asking you not to respond until every person in the group has spoken."

I turned to J.T. and let him begin. After he finished, Bob was next. Flip then read his letter, which was fascinating. He had been with Curtis on and off for thirty years. During the early stages of their career, they had used drugs and drank together often. Eight years earlier, Flip had stopped using any drugs, including caffeine or nicotine. He talked in his letter about some of their early escapades that even Mary was unaware of. After Flip finished, Curtis began to grow visibly upset. He seemed sad instead of angry, and I debated whether or not to even continue. He was actually quite pitiful. Apparently the entire Tucumcari experience had overwhelmed him. Yet, I had seen this reaction before in others and given in prematurely.

Margaret and Fred were next, then his mother, Miriam. After she finished, Curtis turned toward me, crying audibly.

"What is it you all want me to do? Hell, I know I'm sick. Do you all want to commit me somewhere? Is that what you want? I don't need to be convinced. I don't need to hear anymore. I know I'm crazy. I'm willing to do whatever I've got to do to get better." Mary, Shannon, and Lacey were reduced to tears. Everyone else in the room was close. I looked around and then turned to Curtis, nodding my head.

"Curtis." I leaned toward him. "You're a very lucky man." J.T., Flip, and Ike had packed a suitcase for him. They took Curtis to the Nashville airport where he boarded a private jet with the engines already running. Flip and Ike flew with him to an alcohol treatment center out west. He remained there five weeks, then went to an Outward Bound program for five weeks. Mary and the children spent almost two weeks in the treatment center with Curtis.

Mary then went through the entire Outward Bound course with him. Afterward they entered marital and individual therapy to complete the work toward finishing business and avoiding the Elvis Syndrome in future.

> *"It is neither wealth nor splendor but tranquillity*
> *and occupation which give happiness."*
> *— Thomas Jefferson*

It is usually best to get a professional involved in these types of interventions. Curtis had hit bottom and was ready, but HAPs are highly resistant and reluctant. If you get support from the appropriate people, the chances of success are quite high. People such as employers, family members, ministers, priests or others the HAP sees as authority figures are generally helpful. It is also quite beneficial to include a peer who has overcome similar problems. Usually, by the time an intervention is necessary, there is not a great deal to lose by attempting it. If the intervention fails, the HAP is not going to get help. Without it, he or she is unlikely to get help as well. I emphasize the importance of consulting a professional before attempting such intervention.

Most people want help but may be shy or scared to admit it. In my experience, most people cope the best they know how.

Without closure, life often becomes a series of repetitive instant replays. Good intentions are never enough because the HAP will relive the same scenario over and over again without any kind of help. Perhaps the players or locations change, but it's the same drama replayed in redundantly familiar patterns.

This was the evolution of MDWIFE when she originally came to see me. It was also the pattern when she came to see me recently. As indicated earlier, she had gone through quite a bit of psychotherapy since the divorce from MD. We had focused on her weight gain as a child. A similar weight gain had occurred during her marriage difficulty and divorce. Immediately prior to her second marriage, she had gone through yet another weight gain. This same tune kept popping up, revealing her way of dealing with the feared intimacy, closeness, and commitment. She had set her thermostat quite low when it came to intimacy. "Nothing is permanent," she had told me. "No person, no place, no thing is permanent. Especially if he has an appendage between his legs! My father wasn't. My ex wasn't. Men simply aren't permanent . . . ."

In her first marriage she had made the same mistake as Topanga Jack. She had focused exclusively outside of herself. Where Topanga Jack had focused on success, MDWIFE had focused on MD. She built her entire life, both internally and externally, around him. It proved to have the same results as Topanga Jack's. It was a mistake of gigantic proportions. But, as she explained, it was exactly what was expected of her. She put him through medical school, became the near perfect doctor's wife, subjugated her will to his, and ended up with nothing.

She began psychotherapy after her divorce, and re-entered it prior to her second marriage. MDWIFE was probably the most ambitious learner I've ever met. She probably did, as she claimed, "put the bastard through school both financially and academically." "I wrote all of his papers," she once reminisced. "I would even spend all night in the medical library doing research for him so he could sleep." As I got to know her, I didn't doubt a word of it. She read more self-help books than I could even identify. She attended my weekend seminar series for over two years, even though they were often repeats. She would call the office to see if I had any cancellations. She wanted to come in for more psychotherapy if possible. I told her one time she should be awarded a master's degree in street counseling!

But there was one big problem that was never overcome. Even after all our work, she still had trouble with intimacy. "Every time I began to get close," she explained, "I put on a couple of layers of fat. Like it was going to protect me or something. I'm like a bear putting on my winter coat. It protects me all right. It runs the guy off." She had set her thermostat at "cold" where closeness was concerned. That seemed to be where she was comfortable. But it wasn't simply a problem of closeness. She had actually never gotten closure with MD, or her father. As long as she was angry with either, there was still some unfinished business. Eventually we were able to work through the problem she had with her father. She was angry at him for moving her around and dislocating her during her childhood. She was also upset at him for leaving her with her mother who had some serious drinking problems. Finally, we were able to work to get closure on those two areas. The only one remaining was her lingering anger toward MD.

"I know," she lamented. "I read about it in a book the other day. But I can't do all that screaming and bataka-bat [a stuffed therapeutic bat used to help people deal with their anger] hitting and all that kind of stuff. It seems so phony to me. It's like something they do out in California or something."

I laughed out loud since I was educated in California. "Well then, do something else," I gestured. "I don't know, beat up your pillow. Throw pencils at the ceiling. Scream. Yell. Kick. Write poetry. Sing a song. I don't care what you do. But you've got to do something to let go of these emotions. If you don't, you're going to be miserable for your entire life. You're going to keep on running people off and you're going to be left miserable and alone. Now, you tell me you want a relationship, but what you do gets just the opposite. That tells me you're still hanging onto feelings about him and frankly you're letting him control your life. You've got to let go."

"I just can't do that," she swore almost defiantly. "I can read. I can go to seminars. I can talk to you. But I just can't do all that emotional work. Even when I have PMS I'm not that bad!" she laughed.

"Well for goodness sake then," I became exasperated, "what can you do?"

Her eyes lit up as she smiled. "I can paint!" she claimed proudly. "I'm a fairly good painter."

"Great!" I raised my hands toward the ceiling. "So paint. Paint how you feel. Paint your emotions. Paint about what he did. How you feel about it. Get all your gear together and put it down on canvas, on paper, or whatever you use. But when you're done, here's the goal. I don't want you to have anything inside here, inside your gut that's not in your painting. Take everything out of here." I gestured toward my midsection. "And put it all out here. Put it all on this painting."

She smiled and started rocking calmly. "Now that's something," she folded her arms, "I can do."

I didn't see MDWIFE for over two weeks. The day she returned for her appointment, I heard LA and Bud oohing and aahing in the waiting room. I went out to see what was going on and there it was, matted in a two-foot by four-foot gold frame, was her finished business. Painted on an off-white canvas were two abstract naked bodies, one sitting behind the other. The rear figure, which appeared masculine, had his arms wrapped around the front figure. Both figures' hands rested in the pubic area of the female figure. The colors were bold blues, greens, reds, and oranges mixed in with the basic background of earth tones. The female figure wore gold-rimmed sunglasses with what appeared to be magazine print on the lenses. There were hundreds of small holes on the canvas, six larger holes and three slashes, all showing the black matting of the background. In gold script various phrases were written, which turned out to be things MD and the scrub nurse had said to each other. MDWIFE had heard tapes of some of their telephone conversations. I stared at it for a few moments, not certain what it was, or what to say. I looked up, first at MDWIFE, then at Bud, and finally at LA. Each smiled at me expectantly.

Finally LA spoke, "It's fabulous!"

"I think it's just wonderful," Bud added.

"I did it this weekend." MDWIFE smiled. "I was so jazzed!"
A few moments of silence followed.
Finally I asked the obvious question. "Are those bullet holes?"
Everyone laughed.
She told the story in the waiting room as we listened. She
grew more enthusiastic as she spoke. "Oh, it was such a relief. I
ran everybody off Saturday and got started in my art room. The
more I painted, the more I cried. Then I started cussing and spit-
ting and stomping. Finally when I got done with the painting, I
was so excited. I took it outside and set it up against a tree and
shot it with my .410 shotgun. Well, that helped, but it wasn't
enough. So then I got my .38 and emptied it. It felt better but still
that wasn't quite enough. So I was blubberin' and cryin' and I
went inside and got a butcher knife and then stabbed it..uh..like
something from "Psycho" till I fell down and just cried in the
backyard. Ever since then I've felt great!"
When I finally asked her what she named it, she answered
with one word that explained her mood upswing. She smiled,
looked at me, while pausing, then she said very softly, *Closure*.
Closure hangs on a wall in my office today.

> *"I detest the man who hides one thing in the depth of his*
> *heart and speaks forth another."*
> —*Homer*, The Iliad

For some reason we respond to rituals. Painting helped
MDWIFE. Once a woman came into my office with taped music
and "danced her feelings" for me. Another time, a guy walked in
with his guitar. He said he couldn't talk about how he felt today,
but he could sing about it. He spent nearly an hour singing various melodies he had written over the weekend. There have been
a few times when I had no idea what people were trying to
express. But when they achieved closure, they knew. And it's
their awareness that has been helpful, not mine.
Much of the negative programming that occurs in childhood
has a profound impact. I see an extremely self-destructive person, and don't really understand why. He or she doesn't understand either. The reason is because that person is responding to

unfinished business that began perhaps when he or she was a toddler. This turned out to be the case with Cow Pies. He recalled the countless messages "You're just like your father." That's not altogether bad. His father had some tremendous qualities. But he also had some less-than-ideal characteristics you may not want to follow. His father had experienced alcohol problems, severe financial problems, and near-violent marital difficulty. If those weren't enough, he had gotten shot down three times as a fighter pilot during the Vietnam War. The last time, tragically, he never returned and was listed missing in action. I knew all of this, but only this, about his father before we had our final ritual.

If "you're just like your father" and he did all of those things, then what would the dutiful son do? Especially if you're named after him, "Cow Pies, Jr." He had done his best to become just like dad, with only a few twists. Cow Pies had experienced various problems with the basics. He destroyed much of his life with alcohol, bad marriages, and terrible financial problems. However, his eyesight had been too bad to become a fighter pilot so he joined the Army and became a Green Beret at age nineteen. There wasn't a "real war" at that time, so he had volunteered and actually been wounded in Iran during the Shah's ouster. The same thing happened in Nicaragua when Somoza was overthrown. He served as a liaison to the British Commandos in the Faulkland campaign. He was one of the first Americans to invade Grenada and was there doing reconnaissance two days before the actual invasion began. He was in the reserves during the last two conflicts, and volunteered for active duty. Two of his previous wives had claimed he had a death wish and left him after he pursued these escapades. Going out of your way to step in cow pies is one thing. But volunteering to get killed or winding up missing in action as a result is totally different.

For the sake of the book, I'm summarizing Cow Pies' events. It took a long time for either of us to realize what actually was happening. When we did, I urged quick action. To me, this was literally of life-and-death importance. A tremendous amount of work by both of us had preceded our attempt to finally seek closure. My opinion was that Cow Pies needed to bury his father and at the same time get permission to live longer than he did.

He also needed to learn how to avoid future piles. My belief was that if we got closure he would no longer be "singing the same tune" and would be able to avoid ambushes in the future. I figured he had stepped in enough piles for one lifetime. We set up an appointment and planned to "bury" his father. Cow Pies had never attended a funeral or memorial service for his dad. The fact one hadn't been arranged seemed quite immoral to me.

He invited his sister, a friend from work, and his girlfriend to join us in the ritual. Since he was Episcopalian, I had planned to read some selections from *The Book of Common Prayer*. A picture of his dad, along with a collection of his medals and flight wings had been set up at a table in my office. The entire series of events were very somber and serious. Our mood was purposefully consistent with a funeral. In this particular ritual a funeral was exactly what was held. The fact that the body was not present was quite irrelevant. The burial was not for the dead person, it was for the living.

I've conducted many funerals in my office over the years. Sometimes we have funerals after divorces and bury the marriage. On another occasion we buried a double amputee's legs in my office. Obviously, his legs were not present for the service. The purpose of such rituals is to formally say "goodbye." It's something many people have forgotten to do. We can say hello quite successfully, but saying goodbye is more difficult. For reasons I'll explain later, the funeral of Cow Pie's father was a little different from most in its content. In its impact, however, it was consistent with many others I've held over the years. It seems the healing actually begins with the ritual. The ritual does not mean the pain is over. It does mean that the formal beginning-of-the-end has occurred.

When you bury someone, you don't simply forget them. In some way, a formal time set aside for grieving eases the transition process. I often suggest it takes a year to bury a person or a marriage. This is because the first anniversary of everything brings many difficulties. The first Christmas without the person, the first New Year's, Thanksgiving, birthday, etc. all bring back a bit of sadness. However, after the first year, if the person continues toward health, things grow easier. Most people never set aside the time for the ritual and seek closure. The ritual is not magic. But sometimes the impact is—in more ways than one.

I never know why people actually come to see me for counseling. In each city where I've lived there have been many competent and well-trained psychotherapists. In Cow Pies' case, he came to see me because I had appeared on his TV station many occasions. Apparently he felt like he knew me and was more comfortable opening up under those circumstances. Some people prefer therapists they don't know at all. Sometimes I think it's divine guidance that brings people together. Regardless, Cow Pies' ritual was filled with eerie coincidences. It was probably the most profound and dramatic burial I have ever conducted. The reasons were quite personal.

As the funeral began, Cow Pies handed me a summary of the government investigation regarding his father's disappearance and asked me to read it. This was supposed to be the opening of the ritual. I took it and began to read. "On June 19th, 1969, as part of Operation Bloody Stilleto, in support of I Corps MACV Forces approximately forty miles north of Chu Lai, South Vietnam F-4 fighters were called to assist." I looked up at the group and set the papers down solemnly. For a few moments I just looked at the floor. When I looked up I wasn't sure what to say but decided finally to tell the truth.

"I was there," I said suddenly. "I was on the ground during Bloody Stilleto. I was part of that operation on June 19th 1969. I'll never forget it because it was the first time I got shot. In fact I called in F-4s for air support. One of them got hit with ground gunfire. It sounded like a .51-caliber. There was a parachute spotted. I saw the chute but I couldn't tell whether the pilot was alive or not. At that point, all hell broke loose! I got hit in the leg. A bunch of people got wounded. One of my good friends got killed in Bloody Stilleto." I continued to tell them all I could remember about the mission. They all stared at me, shocked.

" Oh, God." his sister sighed. "What's today's date?"

"June 19th" a friend responded. It was June 19, 1985. We were conducting the ritual sixteen years to the day after his father was shot down. On that very day Cow Pies was sixteen years old. I was nineteen years old.

The number of coincidences continued. It turned out to be a highly emotional time for all of us. Due to the circumstances, we all joined in the grieving. Frankly, I probably grieved longer than anyone. I may have been the last American to see his father alive, if in fact it was him, and if in fact he was alive. I may have spoken to him on the radio. We will never know. What we do know is that his son truly began getting better on that day. Sixteen years to the day after he was shot down. I was there on both occasions.

> *"Our remedies oft in ourselves do lie."*
> —*Shakespeare,* All's Well That Ends Well

As a result of the ritual we completed, MDWIFE ultimately was able to reset her thermostat. I literally designed a ritual around her visualizing an internal "intimacy thermostat" and had her turn it up to about ninety degrees. She reported hearing the furnace kick on, and now it's quite apparent her intimacy temperature is a lot higher. Cow Pies ultimately buried his father as well as the negative programming. It has been a struggle for him, but he's actually been able to avoid a number of opportunities to step in new piles. One was Desert Storm, which he didn't go to. And the good news is he felt no guilt or temptation to go either.

You can get healthier. You can learn to avoid death by success. Sometimes it's a struggle to avoid the Elvis Syndrome. But you can survive. Talented vocalist and performer Michael McDonald overcame his own set of obstacles and is still productive long after the death by success of Steely Dan, and the Doobie Brothers. Michael's story, in fact, was one of the inspirations to write this book. He overcame his problems and continued to be creatively productive. Jerry Lee Lewis is another example of someone who is still alive and productive after his own brushes with death by success. The number of singers, actors, and athletes who have avoided death by success is far greater than those who haven't.

The reality is, you can learn new patterns of behavior and survive. Or you can continue with unfinished tunes and keep humming them over and over again until they ultimately destroy you.

Like many others, Curtis chose to change his tune. After his formal psychotherapy and treatment, he has continued to lead a healthy life. He also has followed Dr. Karl Menninger's advice and helped dozens of other people "more depressed than himself". He still records and performs at concerts. After completing the first draft of this book, I gave him a weekend to review it. We met halfway between Nashville and Chattanooga several days later. We decided to go for a walk near the campus of the University of the South in Sewanee. We had done this on several occasions before and enjoyed the beautiful mountain scenery.

"Well," he reached over and patted me on the back. "The book is great. I really think a lot of people can benefit from it. I guess there will be some people from Nashville who recognize me. But I really don't care about that. The ones who would recognize me already know my story anyway. People will read that book. It'll really help 'em."

"Thanks a lot," I responded. "I guess I do hope people will read it. If they won't read it, we'll come up with some tapes or something, and maybe they'll just listen to it."

"Oh, by the way," Curtis interrupted me, "you know I have diversified now. You emphasized that to me on several different occasions, and when I got to that part of the book I recognized what you were talking about. I have done that."

"Yeah," I nodded my head. "I know you have. I'm not worried about that anymore."

"Well," Curtis continued as we headed toward his favorite trail, "I just wanted you to know I'd done it. I also like that part in there about the difference between happiness and success. You know, I'd never thought about it until I read that. There is a huge difference between those two. We ought to learn that a whole lot younger."

"Definitely," I nodded my head in agreement. "You're both of those now, aren't you? You're successful and happy both. Isn't it great?"

"Yeah," he sighed. "Yeah, I guess so. I know I'm happy. And I guess I'm successful too. By most measurements I guess I'm both. How about you?"

"Happy? Definitely." I responded quickly. "Successful? No,

not as much as I'd like to be. I guess I'm successful by some people's standards. I would like to be able to pay my bills on time every once in a while." We both laughed out loud.

"You'll get that." He smiled at me paternally. "You just keep on writing. That's what you need to be doing. Don't stop like you did before. I think you just gave up at one point in your life and that was probably a big mistake. You keep on writing and you'll get all the success you can handle. And probably more."

"No," I laughed. "I'm not going to Elvis-out on you."

"I know." Curtis laughed. "So how're you gonna end the book?

"I don't know." I shook my head. "It's the hardest part. I'm gonna write an epilogue and tie all the loose ends together. Kind of get closure on everything."

"By the way," Curtis continued. "What are you gonna do for an encore this time? I know the book's been a big deal in your life. So what are you gonna do now?" He stopped again while looking at me, without smiling. "What are you going to do for an encore?"

I shrugged my shoulders. "Well, we've already talked about it. I think we're probably gonna put the stuff in a big envelope Monday and take it to Federal Express. Tuesday we're taking a day off. Sometime Tuesday we'll say goodbye to this book. And Wednesday we'll start on an entirely different one."

Curtis smiled and placed his arm on my shoulder. "Different tune, huh?" I nodded my head as we continued walking.

JOURNAL SESSION

1. If you're like most Americans, there are probably several areas in your life where you have not achieved closure. You may think you don't have any. That's part of the problem. In our work as consultants we've never sat down with anyone to seriously investigate their life without finding closure problems. Be painfully honest with yourself and list two or three areas of your life, or events of your life where you have not achieved closure. Don't worry about closure. Just be honest about the fact that you haven't achieved it.

2. You may have decided not to think about your ex-husband or wife. However, every time your mind is free to wander you find yourself thinking about him. He's even in your dreams. Rather than decide not to think about him anymore, the key is to "bury" him. Sometimes this has to be done more than once. Describe your experience with the phenomenon "that which is repressed, is expressed."

3. Describe a time when you may have made the same mistake as Topanga Jack and MDWIFE—focusing on externals. Describe the results.

4. Our society has lost most of its rituals. That's unfortunate. We believe rituals are very important. Take a moment to describe rituals in your life that you'd like to re-install. Make one ritual a daily ritual, one a weekly ritual, one a monthly ritual, and one an annual ritual. Feel free to use standard rituals such as church, Christmas, etc.

CHECKLIST

Directions: Give yourself a grade (A-F) for each of the items below.

___1. I've done a good job letting go of old remnants of past behavior that have become problematic in my life.

___2. I'm well aware of the programming that occurred in my childhood and have discussed it with another person.

___3. I have developed an understanding that it takes quite a period of time to break old habits. I understand that mere awareness alone will not achieve the needed breakthrough.

___4. I have made a list of areas in my life where I need to pursue closure. I have made further plans to arrange for the closure needed.

___5. I have made a point of talking with friends or relatives who could act as lifeguards. I have given them permission to confront me and suggested ways and means they might use to intervene when they see me involved in negative patterns of behavior.

_____6. I have found an acceptable way to let go of negative emotions in my life. Similar to MDWIFE I am able to express emotions I repressed in the past.

_____7. I have developed various rituals in my life to help me stay emotionally balanced.

_____8. I actually believe I can change destructive behavior from the past.

_____9. If I had a friend who I felt was Elvising out, I would be willing to force the issue and participate in a confrontation.

_____10. I've made an effort to cultivate healthy relationships in my life, either with current friends and family or by seeking new acquaintances.

ELVIS HAS LEFT THE BUILDING
EPILOGUE

"Everything which is properly business we must keep carefully separate from life. Business requires earnestness and method; life must have a freer handling."
— Goethe

One of the interesting stories Curtis told me had to do with a pendant he said Priscilla had designed for Elvis. The pendant was a gold lightning bolt surrounded by the initials T.C.B. The C was in the center and top of the lightning bolt and attached to a gold necklace. The initials, T.C.B., stood for Take Care of Business. The slogan became one of the King's mottos; he encouraged people to take care of business—to focus on getting the job at hand done. The story is he gave this pendant to close members of his entourage whom he really trusted. But to me, T.C.B. has another meaning. It means Time to Change Beliefs.

Within a year after the funeral ritual, Cow Pies returned to my office. On multiple occasions he had written or called me, ecstatic at having avoided another pie. He had learned to miss the obvious ones. Yet over the course of time, he occasionally tripped into new and different messes.

"I don't walk a mile out of my way to wallow into a pile of cow pies like I used to," he explained. "Yet I still end up in them from time to time. Now—it's more like something can look really great, but then when I actually get in the situation I realize it's just another cow pie. And I can end up in a mess up to my elbows! Then I bust my buns and end up smelling like a rose once again. But it's the same process.

"The problem is, now it's much more subtle. I mean they used to be obvious—now they're not. The messes are smaller, I admit. But there still have been a couple of bad ones. What I really want to know is—will I ever get over this crap for good?"

His question was both sincere and profound. And frankly it's one that has puzzled and challenged psychotherapists for years. He had progressed. Cow Pies no longer thought he had to repeat his father's death. The pattern was so thoroughly programmed into his subconscious, however, it took tremendous energy to continually avoid it. As we continued our discussion, I began to realize the mistake I had made.

We had removed most of his old beliefs through the ritual. That was an important step. He no longer believed he had to be like his father. The problem was we had not instilled a set of new beliefs. The old beliefs had been removed, but not replaced. He was definitely off the old path. But he was not on a new one. So it was quite easy for him to stray back to the old behavior occasionally.

Behavior change is relatively simple. Changing what you do is not complex. You don't have to enter psychotherapy to quit putting your hand in a waffle iron. Sandwich your hand in a waffle iron a time or two, and you will soon give up the habit. Similarly, you don't have to jump off of an eight-story building to figure out it might hurt. You can look over the edge, contemplate the consequences, and decide "not today." For many people, it's equally easy to give up any self-destructive behavior. The consequences themselves are harsh enough to cause you to quit. The change Cow Pies needed to make, however, was deeper. He needed to change beliefs.

A young lady who visited me several years ago in psychotherapy dramatically demonstrated the importance of beliefs. A daughter of American missionaries, she was born, educated, and socialized in an indigenous Japanese community. She went to regular Japanese schools, spoke Japanese as a first language, and truly believed she was Japanese. Since her parents were American, she looked like an American. Yet on the inside, she was completely Japanese. When attempting to attend college in the United States, she experienced tremendous difficulty adjusting and gave an eloquent explanation of why.

"In my mind I'm Japanese. I think in Japanese. I dream in Japanese. When I listen to people speaking English, I translate it into Japanese, think about it, formulate the answer in Japanese, translate it back into English, and then respond. On the outside I'm American. On the inside I'm Japanese. I'm Japanese and nothing has ever changed that for me. I really am who I believe."

The problem for Cow Pies was we had removed the old belief but not replaced it. Instilling a new beliefs system about who he was became a major turning point. Through an elaborate series of psychotherapeutic maneuvers we were able to help him change at the belief level as well. Afterward he discontinued formal psychotherapy. We've continued to speak over the years by telephone and see each other occasionally. His change was complete.

Elvis Presley's appearance changed over the years. His singing styles changed as well. The people around him periodically changed. But the basic core belief Elvis held true about himself never changed. As a result of that belief, he died. Elvis didn't take care of business. And he didn't do the other thing the initials stand for: Time to Change Beliefs. If Elvis would have done that, he may have celebrated his sixtieth birthday in January 1995.

"Keep changing. When you're through changing, you're through."
—Bruce Barton

Another way to take care of business is through closure. It's a very important part of taking care of business. I introduced many people to you in this book. It's important to take care of business as far as they are concerned and bring closure to their stories. It's time to say "goodbye" to them.

As indicated in the last chapter, Curtis is doing quite well. He is very successful both personally and professionally. He regularly gives concerts, makes records, and continues to be tremendously helpful to people both inside and outside the music industry. He and Mary are still married and claim to be very happy.

The last time I spoke to her, MDWIFE was still married to her second husband. She said she still struggles with obesity, but described herself as ". . . ecstatically happy." MD's marriage to the scrub nurse didn't last. He recently went through his third divorce.

Cow Pies still works in television. He's currently an anchorman in a large southern city. The last time we spoke, he was doing far better financially. He continues to avoid the piles of cow mess. I talk to Topanga Jack often. He is involved with various people in business ventures and claims he has found happiness as well as success. He is still married and has experienced tremendous success in resort development. He no longer has a drinking problem, but his wife described him during our last conversation as a recovering workaholic. The Sin Eater, "Father Tim," is now Dr. Tim. He's on the faculty at a community college in Southern California. Tim went through in-patient treatment for alcoholism and has been sober for over eight years.

Bob, the field goal kicker, is now a fireman. He lives in the same town where he went to high school, and has unfortunately given up aspirations of being a professional football player. Tammy, the creative lady, has grown to be very successful. She recently worked as a studio musician on several record projects. She said on the telephone she is very happy as long as there is a creative project for her. St. Louis talk show brother has grown comfortable with more than mediocrity. He recently survived a major job promotion! He's still married and claims to be quite happy.

The couple who smoked marijuana together did get a divorce. I was unable to contact her. I did speak to the husband and he claims marijuana is now just a bad memory. Janey wouldn't return my telephone call. Ron left the family business and has gone out on his own. He and Janey are married but continue to have problems. Since he left the family business, money has been a major problem. Janey has tremendous difficulty with her financial situation, and Ron says "she blames Dr. Baucom for that!" He says he's not rich or successful, but he is happy and that's okay with him. Janey is neither rich, successful, nor happy. Tom, the sixties rock star, is involved in activities other than music and says he is quite satisfied. At the writing of this book, Steve was still in jail. Nanny died several years after Grandpa. She left us tremendous love, wonderful memories, and some beautiful quilts. We are grateful.

> *"Do not wait for the last judgment. It takes place every day."*
> *—Albert Camus*

Most people respond to life. They don't live. They react. I honestly believe ninety-nine percent of the world's population is on automatic pilot. Programming takes over and people respond as robots to some predetermined script. This is one of the tragedies of our existence in the late twentieth century. And it's totally unnecessary. People who don't follow this programming are the ones who make contributions far beyond the norm.

Until the day his mother died, Elvis was truly alive. He was young, dangerous, and profane for his era. Elvis changed the pulse of the world. He didn't respond. He created! He woke people up! He shook America from its apathy as surely as he shook his hips. Young people copied him, and older people feared him. Sadly, too few people understood him.

When Elvis conducted concerts, the building would still be mobbed long after the concert had concluded. The crowd waited for the chance to see, or maybe even touch, Elvis. After he was surreptitiously whisked away, an announcer's voice would come booming over the PA system. "ELVIS HAS LEFT THE BUILDING. ELVIS HAS LEFT THE BUILDING." It was an attempt to encourage the crowd to leave.

Maybe we need to hear it again. *Elvis has left the building.* There's tremendous unfinished business about his life and death. Elvis, like Michael Jordan, left his career at the peak. Unlike Michael, he didn't have the opportunity to say goodbye. That is the tragedy. He didn't know how to diversify. At his death, I truly believe, he was simply tired. He was ready to say goodbye but didn't know how. For whatever reason, in my opinion, the greatest part of him died with his mother. His biological death was more an afterthought. As a result, literally millions of fans never got to complete the tune. They need to.

Elvis has left the building.

Many people need to face it and say goodbye. The legacy of his music continues. His other legacy is learning to overcome death by success. It is my belief that anyone who experiences the Elvis Syndrome can overcome it. I have experienced it in my own life more than once. It's likely, everyone has. If you follow the principles discussed in this book, you can avoid it in the future. For whatever reason during Elvis's life, the understanding of how to avoid death by success did not exist. Today it does.

In one of my first visits with Curtis he made several astute observations. One of them was that Elvis's entourage "did everything possible to save his career, but not a damn thing to save his life." Another observation was that Elvis and people like him don't need bodyguards, they need lifeguards. The first statement probably is unfair. The second one, however, is understated. Though the truth will probably never be known, I would imagine his entourage did all they could to save Elvis's life. It simply was not enough, though there was little else they could have done. And Curtis was right. He did need lifeguards. Probably many of us do. Like most people, Elvis was his own worst enemy.

The "technology" of psychotherapy, such as it is, was not well-developed at the time Elvis was alive. If he had gone through a confrontation similar to the kind we did with Curtis, Elvis probably would have responded to it. There was nothing torturing him so severely he could not have been helped. The awareness simply wasn't there to Take Care of Business. This is one of the tragedies of Elvis's death. It is also one of the reasons we as Americans have had such difficulty letting go.

"However mean your life is, meet it and live it; do not shun and call it hard names. It is not so bad as you are. It looks poorest when you are richest. The fault finder will find faults even in paradise. Love your life."
— Thoreau

Elvis was a dichotomy. He represents the psychological dichotomy within each of us. He was shy but profane, naive yet brilliantly creative, a true country boy but worldly wise. It was on his jet, the *Lisa Marie*, that Priscilla reportedly designed the

T.C.B. lightning bolt pendant. It was a happier time, then. Perhaps her real message to Elvis was hauntingly prophetic. "Take Care of Business, Elvis. Take care of the real business, before it's too late—before we all have to say goodbye." She sent the message far more directly later. Had Elvis listened, he could have avoided death by success.

Just as many others need to say goodbye to Elvis, far more need to say goodbye to the Elvis Syndrome. Regardless of the form—from alcoholism or drug abuse to destructive relationships to suicidal tendencies—you can say goodbye. Elvis's life, death, and legacy can show you how to improve your life.

"Elvis has left the building."

"Thankyouverymuch."

T.C.B.

ABOUT THE AUTHOR

John Q. Baucom, Ph.D., is a psychotherapist with a counseling practice in Chattanooga, Tennessee. He is the author of *Fatal Choice: The Teenage Suicide Crisis; Help Your Children Say No to Drugs*; and *Bonding and Breaking Free: What Every Parent Should Know.*

Dr. Baucom has appeared on national radio and television, including *Hour Magazine, Good Morning America*, and *Sally Jesse-Raphael*. He also has been featured in Japan, Germany, Great Britain, and Russia. Currently he hosts his own call-in radio show.

WELL-KNOWN HAPs

HAPs Who Have Died

Marilyn Monroe—actress, died at age thirty-six of barbiturate overdose. It was ruled a possible suicide.

Humphrey Bogart—actor, died at age fifty-eight of cancer. Heavy drinking and smoking were contributing factors.

James Dean—actor, died at age twenty-four in a high-speed automobile accident.

Janis Joplin—rock and blues singer, died at age twenty-seven from a heroin overdose.

Howard Hughes—industrialist billionaire, died at age seventy-one of unknown causes. He lived his last few years in a hermit's existence and was deathly afraid of germs and bacteria.

Rock Hudson—the actor, died at age sixty of AIDS. He was the first major public figure that admitted contracting HIV.

Jimi Hendrix—rock singer and guitarist, died at age twenty-seven of a heroin overdose.

F. Scott Fitzgerald—famous writer, died at age forty-four of an apparent heart attack. He was a heavy drinker and smoker.

Ernest Hemingway—died at age sixty-two of a self-inflicted shotgun blast.

Vincent Van Gogh—painter, died at age thirty-seven of a self-inflicted gunshot wound.

Judy Garland—actress and singer, died at age forty-seven of a drug overdose.

W.C. Fields—actor and comedian, died at age sixty-seven of complications brought on by advanced alcoholism.

Lenny Bruce — 1960s counter-culture comedian, died at age thirty-nine of a drug overdose.

Hank Williams Sr. — country singer, died at age thirty of alcohol-related heart disease.

John Belushi — actor, comedian, and singer, died at age thirty-three of a drug overdose.

Lyle Alzedo — NFL all-pro defensive lineman, died at age forty-three of brain cancer. He felt that steroids, which he had taken for over twenty years, contributed to this cancer.

Kurt Cobain — Nirvana singer and songwriter, died at age twenty-seven of a self-inflicted shotgun blast. Heroin and Valium were found in his system.

Jim Henson — *Muppets* puppeteer, died at age fifty-four of bronchial pneumonia, which he ignored until hospitalized.

John Candy — actor and comedian, died at age forty-four of a heart attack. He weighed well over three hundred pounds.

River Phoenix — Academy Award-nominated actor, died at age twenty-three from injecting bad heroin.

Freddie Prinze — star of the T.V. series *Chico and the Man*, died at age twenty-two of a self-inflicted gunshot wound.

Sam Kennison — movie actor and stand-up comedian, died in an automobile accident five days after his wedding.

Richard Milhous Nixon — former president, died at age eighty-one of natural causes. He was the only United States president forced to resign office.

Len Bias — successful basketball player at the University of Maryland who died of a cocaine overdose after being selected in the first round draft by the Boston Celtics. Bias had a lifelong dream to play for the Celtics.

Jim Morrison — The Doors' lead singer. Died in Paris at age twenty-eight under mysterious circumstances.

Jim Jones — charismatic evangelist known to his followers as the Reverend Jim Jones. Formed a cult in San Francisco and eventually moved it to Guyana where Jones and 913 of his followers committed suicide.

David Koresh — messianic leader of the military/religious Branch Davidians, located in Waco, Texas. When federal authorities attempted to search the Davidian compound for illegal weapons, an exchange of gunfire resulted in many Davidians, including Koresh, being killed.

Jim Fixx—noted author and pioneer of the running movement. He ignored complaints of chest pain and other problems, continued to run, and suffered a fatal heart attack.

HAPs Who Are Living

Gary Hart—senator and presidential candidate, forced out of the race and his office when he was caught in marital infidelity with Donna Rice.

Pete Rose—all-star baseball player and manager. He developed addictive gambling problems that ended his career and destroyed his family.

Jimmy Swaggart—televangelist who took in more than twelve million dollars per month at one time in his career but destroyed it all by fighting with fellow evangelists and being caught with prostitutes on two separate occasions.

Wilbur Mills—powerful congressman who was driven from office after repeatedly making drunken displays of affection toward stripper Fanny Fox in public.

Jim Bakker—former multi-millionaire televangelist who drugged and coerced Jessica Hahn into having sex with him. He gave her six-figure payoffs to remain silent. The discovery of this led to his downfall and eventual imprisonment.

Rob Lowe—film actor, caught with a sexually explicit videotape involving himself and an underage female.

Edward M. Kennedy—senator, first elected in 1962 at age thirty. His political standing was damaged by his conduct in the 1969 drowning of Mary Jo Kopeckne at Chappaquiddick, Massachusettes.

Derrick Sanderson—National Hockey League star. He signed a two million dollar contract at age twenty-six. Shortly thereafter, he virtually self-destructed trying to live up to the image he felt he had to maintain.

Mickey Monus—Phar-Mor discount drug chain founder. Within ten years Phar-Mor had grown into a three billion dollar company. When Monus was fired, he faced one hundred twenty-nine counts of fraud and other charges, and Phar-Mor was thrown into Chapter Eleven bankruptcy.

Michael Milken—"big hitter" in insider-trading scandals. Earned one billion dollars in a four-year period. Sentenced to ten years in jail and six hundred million dollars in fines.

Ivan Boesky—stock trader who used insider-trading information. At arrest he was said to be worth more than two-hundred million. Fined over one-hundred million dollars and two years in jail.

Dennis Levine—investment banker for Drexl-Burnam. He earned two million dollars per year and yet he got involved in illegal insider trading where he made an additional twelve million. Caught in 1986, he served seventeen months in a minimum security prison.

Martin Segal—merger specialist at Drexl-Kidder-Peabody who took payments from Ivan Boesky for insider tips. After he implicated Boesky and several others, Segal received the lightest sentence serving only two months.

Leona Helmsley—real-estate billionaire convicted on several counts of tax evasion, embezzlement, and extortion. After her conviction and imprisonment it was determined that she owed less than one percent of her net worth.

Jerry Lee Lewis—early rock 'n' roll star of the fifties, fell into disfavor with his fans for marrying his thirteen-year-old cousin. Problems with drugs and alcohol, the mysterious deaths of two of his wives, and troubles with the Internal Revenue Service (IRS) have plagued Jerry Lee in recent years.

James Watt—secretary of the interior in the Reagan administration, was removed from office for inappropriate statements made to the press. In the late eighties, Watt working as a private citizen used his access to top Housing and Urban Development (HUD) officials to earn four hundred twenty thousand dollars in fees for winning valuable housing contracts.

Sam Pierce—HUD Secretary in the Reagan Administration. Congressional findings show that four billion to eight billion dollars were lost through mismanagement and fraud during his tenure.

Willie Nelson—country music artist. He was investigated by the IRS and found to owe over fourteen million dollars in back taxes. Many of his assets were seized. But after years of tours and an album whose proceeds were sent to the IRS, Willie eventually paid his debt. Allegations of marijuana use have surfaced recently

Marion Barry—mayor of Washington D.C., who was caught in a government sting operation when he was videotaped buying and using crack cocaine in 1990. He was re-elected in 1994.

George Jones—legendary country music singer He eventually became known as " No-Show" when alcoholism caused him to miss many of his performances and badly damaged his career.

Darryl Strawberry—Major League Baseball outfielder. He fell into cocaine addiction after observing teammate Dwight Gooden's stellar pitching season while abusing cocaine. Later Strawberry said, "Success is great, but then everything hits the fan."

Brian Wilson—driving force behind The Beach Boys. He began using LSD and other drugs and by 1983 weighed more than three hundred pounds. Placed under the care Dr. Eugene Landy who also became his business manager, executive producer, and musical partner. Ultimately, the state of California took Landy's license for his activities associated with Brian's treatment.

Mike Tyson—heavyweight champion boxer. Unable to control his violent temper outside of the ring, he was charged with rape, convicted, and has just completed his prison sentence.

Paul Reubens—better known as " Pee-Wee Herman" He was caught exposing himself in an adult movie theater in Sarasota, Florida. His subsequent arrest destroyed the character of Pee-Wee Herman, star of the Saturday morning kids' show and several movies.

Steve Howe—Major League Baseball pitcher and Cy Young Award winner. He was repeatedly caught using cocaine and ultimately banned from baseball for life.

Chuck Berry—rock 'n' roll pioneer from the 1950s and 60s who had numerous run-ins with the law. Most recently he was tried and convicted of illegal sexual activity with a minor.

David Crosby—a member of the successful musical groups "Crosby, Stills, Nash, and Young," and "Crosby, Stills, and

Nash." He was convicted at age forty-four of drug possession and went to prison for several years in Texas.

Roger Smith—former CEO of General Motors, featured in a 1989 film titled *Roger and Me*, depicting indifference to the layoffs of thousand of General Motors' workers in Flint, Michigan. He retired in 1990.

BIBLIOGRAPHY

"Addictive Disorders Trap Millions," *USA Today*, January 1992.

"Aloneness, Alcohol, and Age," *Newsweek*, p. 54, December 7, 1992.

Baird, Woody, "Elvis' Early Days on the Road," Associated Press, August 14, 1993.

Balkin, Joseph, "Contributions of Family to Men's Fear of Success in College," *Psychological Reports*, 59:1071-1074, 1986.

BBC Raycon, "Elvis' Life and Times," 1993, *London Times*, August 17, 1977.

Bhogle, Sudha and Vinoda N. Murthy, "Fear of Success in the Indian Context," *The Journal of Personality and Clinical Studies*, 6:35-41, March, 1990.

Blankenship, Virginia, "A Computer-Based Measure of Resultant Achievement Motivation," *Journal of Personality and Social Psychology*, 53:361-372, August, 1987.

Bugliosi, Vincent and Curt Gentry, *Helter Skelter*, New York, Bantam, 1975.

Buss, A. H., *Psychopathology*, New York, Wiley, 1966.

Cadoret, R. J., "Psychopathology in Adopted-away Offspring of Biologic Parents with Anti-social Behavior," *Archives of General Psychiatry*, 35:176-184, 1978.

Clance, Pauline R. and Maureen A. O'Toole, "The Impostor Phenomenon: An Internal Barrier to Empowerment and Achievement," *Women and Therapy*, 6:51-64, Fall, 1987.

Cleckly, H., *The Mask of Sanity*, 4th ed., St. Louis, C. B. Mosby, 1964.

"The Crooner Connection," *Newsweek* , August 17, 1992.

"Dodgers' Strawberry Arrested," Associate Press, Sunday, September 5, 1993.

Eisen, Jonathan, *The Age of Rock*, New York, Random House, 1969

Fleeman, Michael, "Boy's Father Linked to Extortion Plot," Associate Press, Saturday, August 28, 1993.

Fontaine, Anne M., "Impact of Social Context on the Relationship Between Achievement Motivation and Anxiety, Expectations or Social Conformity," *Personality and Individual Differences*, 12:457-466, 1991.

Frank, G., *The Boston Strangler*, New York, New American Library, 1966.

Freud, S., Beyond the Pleasure Principle (1920), N. J. Strachey, ed., *The Standard Edition of the Complete Psychological Works of Sigmund Freud*, Vol. XDIII. London: The Hogarth Press, 1953

Freud, S., *The Ego and the Id* (1923), London: The Hogarth Press, 1947.

Freeman, Lucy and Eddie Jaffe, *Why Norma Jean Killed Marilyn Monroe*, Chicago, Triumph Books, 1992.

Fried-Buchalter, Sharon, "Fear of Success, Fear of Failure, and the Impostor Phenomenon: A Factor Analytic Approach to Convergent and Discriminant Validity," *The Journal of Personality Assessment*, 58:368-379, April 1992.

Friedman, M. and R. H. Rosenman, *Type A Behavior and Your Heart*, New York, Knopf, 1974.

Friedman, P.R., "Mental Retardation and the Law: Report on the Status of Current Cases," Journal of Clinical and Child Psychology, 2(1):37-39, 1971.

Goldman, Albert, "Down at the End of Lonely Street," *Life Magazine*, June 1990.

Gray, J. A., *The Neuropsychology of Anxiety*, New York, Oxford University Press, 1982.

Greer, S., "Study of Parental Loss in Neurotics and Sociopaths," *Archives of General Psychiatry*, 11:177-180, 1964.

Holmes, T. H. and R. H. Rhae, "The Social Readjustment Rating Scale," *Journal of Psychosomatic Research*, 14:121-132, 1970.

Holmes, T. S. and T. H. Holmes, "Short Term Intrusions into the

Lifestyle Routine," *Journal of Psychosomatic Research*, 14:121-132.

Horino, Midori, The Relation Between Achievement Motive and Fear of Success," *The Japanese Journal of Psychology*, 62:255-259, October, 1991.

Hyland, Michael E., "There is No Motive to Avoid Success: The Compromise Explanation for Success-Avoiding Behavior," *Journal of Personality*, 57:665-693, September, 1989.

Ishiyama, F., et al, "Birth Order and Fear of Success Among Midadolescents," *Psychological Reports*, 66:17-18, February, 1990.

Ivins, Molly, "Elvis Presley Dies, Rock Singer was 42," *New York Times*, August 17, 1977.

Janman, Karen, "Achievement Motivation Theory and Occupational Choice," *The European Journal of Social Psychology*, 17:327-346, July-September 1987.

Jellinek, E. N., *Phases in the Drinking History of Alcoholics*, New Haven, Conn.: Yale House Press, 1946.

Krausner, L. and L. P. Alman, *Behavior Influence and Personality: The Social Matrix of Human Action*, New York, Holt, Rinehart and Winston, 1973.

Krogh, Egil, *The Day Elvis Met Nixon*, Bellvue, Wash., Pajama Press, 1994.

Krueger, David W., "Achievement Inhibition in Contemporary Women: Developmental Considerations," *Hillside Journal of Clinical Psychiatry*, 10:232-243, Fall-Winter, 1988.

Lacocque, Pierre E., "An Existential Interpretation of Success Neurosis," *Journal of Religion and Health*, 25:96-106, 1986.

Larkin, Linda, "Identity and Fear of Success," *Journal of Counseling Psychology*, 34:38-45, January 1987.

Littig, Lawrence W., "Motivation and Class Mobility in England: Longitudinal Evidence of a Causal Relationship," *Social Behavior and Personality*, 18:81-86, 1990.

Llaneza-Ramoz, Maria L., "Perceived Gender and Drive for Success," *Phillipine Journal of Psychology*, 24:59-64, June, 1991.

Lykken, D.T., "A Study of Anxiety in the Sociopathic Personality," *Journal of Abnormal and Social Psychology*, 55(1):6-10, 1957.

Maher, B. A., *Principles of Psychopathology*, New York, McGraw-Hill, 1956.

Martz, Larry and Robert Parry, "A Slap on the Wrist for Ollie," *Newsweek* , July 17, 1989.

McNiel, E. B., *The Psychoses*, Inglewood Cliffs, N.J., New Jersey-Hall, 1970

McNiel, E. B., *The Quiet Furies*, Inglewood Cliffs, New Jersey, N.J., Hall, 1957.

Mednick, Martha T., "On the Politics of Psychological Constructs: Stop the Bandwagon, I Want to Get Off," *American Psychologist*, 44:1118-1123, August 1989.

Paoli, Ugo, *Rome: Its People and Customs*, New York, D. McKay Company, 1963.

Pedersen, Darhl M. and Tracy Conlin, "Shifts in Fear of Success in Men and Women from 1968 to 1987," *Psychological Reports*, 61:36-38, August, 1987.

Powers, Stephen, et al, "Achievement Motivation and Attributions for Success and Failure," *Psychological Reports*, 57:751-754, December, 1985.

Presley, Priscilla *Beaulieu, Elvis and Me*, Memphis, Thorndike Press, 1985.

Raglan, B. R. and R. J. Brand, "Type A Behavior and Mortality from Coronary Heart Disease," *The New England Journal of Medicine*, 318:65-69, 1988.

Ray, J. J., "Some Cross-Cultural Explorations of the Relationship Between Achievement Motivation and Anxiety," *Personality and Individual Differences*, 11:91-93, 1990.

Robins, E., J. Glassner, J. Keyes, R. Wilkinson, and G. E. Murphy, "The Communication of Suicidal Intent: A Study of 134 Successful (Completed) Suicides," *American Journal of Psychiatry*, 115:724-733, 1959.

Robins, N. L., *Deviant Children Grow Up*, Baltimore, Williams and Wilkins, 1966.

Rockwell, John, "Presley Gave Rock Its Style," *New York Times*, August 17, 1977.

"(Roger and Me) Redux," *Newsweek* , October 5, 1992.

Rusinova, Veselina, "Psychological Regulation of Tension in Work," *Studia Psychologica*, 32:163-171, 1990.

Salzman, L., "Psychotherapeutic Management of Obsessive-Compulsive Patients," *American Journal of Psychotherapy*, 39:323-330, 1985.

Sancho, Ana M.and Jay Hewitt, "Questioning Fear of Success," *Psychological Reports*, 67:803-806, December, 1990.

Santucci, Rebecca, et al, "Fear of Success: Influence of Sex, Year, and Program in College," *Psychological Reports*, 64:551-555, April 1989.

Schachter, S. and B. Latane, "Crime, Cognition and the Autonomic Nervous System," N. D Levine, ed., Nebraska Symposium on Motivation, Vol. 12, Lincoln, University of Nebraska Press, 1954.

Scullard, H. H., *Festivals and Ceremonies of the Roman Republic*, Ithaca, N.Y., Cornell University Press, 1981.

Senchak, Marilyn and Ladd Wheeler, "Fear of Success in the Social Domain," *Journal of Social and Clinical Psychology*, 6:398-407, 1988.

Sherman, Julia A., "Achievement Related Fears: Gender Roles and Individual Dynamics. Special Issue: Treating Women's Fear of Failure," *Women and Therapy*, 6:97-105, Fall, 1987.

Singh, Satvir and Jaskaran Kaur, "Motive to Avoid and Approach Success: Two Dimensions of the Same Motive," *Asian Journal of Psychology and Education*, 19:1-7, January, 1987.

Steinberg, Warren, "The Fear of Success," Quadrant, 20:23-39, 1987.

Suarez-Orozco, Marcelo M., "'Becoming Somebody': Central American Immigrants in U. S. Inner City Schools Special Issue: Explaining the School Performance of Minority Students," *Anthropology and Education Quarterly* , 18:287-299, December, 1987.

Swain, Austin and Graham Jones, "Relationships Between Sport Achievement Orientation and Competitive State Anxiety," *Sport Psychologist*, 6:42-54, March, 1992.

Volkmer, R. E. and N. T. Feather, "Relations Between Type A Scores, Internal Locus of Control and Test Anxiety," Personality and Individual Differences, 12:205-209, 1991.

Wagner, D. N., D. J. Schneider, S. R. Carter, and T. L. White, (1987) "Paradoxical Effects of Thought Suppression," *Journal of Personality and Social Psychology*, 53:13.

Waters, Harry F., et al, "A Queen on Trial," *Newsweek* Magazine, August 21, 1989.

Weinstein, K. A., G. P. Davidson, E. De-Quattro, and J. W.Allen, "Type A Behavior and Cognitions: Is Hostility the Bad Actor?" Presented at the annual Convention of the American Psychological Association, Washington, D.C., 1986.

Wicks-Nelson, R. and A. C. Israel, *Behavior Disorders of Childhood*, Inglewood Cliffs, N.J.: Prentice-Hall, 1984.

Williams and Wilkins, *Modern Synopsis of Comprehensive Textbook of Psychiatry*, IV, 4th Ed., Baltimore, 1985

Yamauchi, Hirotsugu, "Factorial Analysis of Achievement-Related Motives Measured by Revised-ARMS," *Psychologia An International Journal of Psychology in the Orient*, 29:72-79, June, 1986.

Zax, N. and G. Strickler, *Patterns of Psychopathology*: Case Studies in Behavioral Dysfunction, New York and London, McMillan, 1963.

INDEX